THE POLITICS OF WORLD HUNGER

HARPER'S
MAGAZINE
PRESS

THE POLITICS OF WORLD HUNGER

Grass-Roots Politics and World Poverty

Paul and Arthur Simon

HARPER'S MAGAZINE PRESS
Published in Association with Harper & Row
New York

THE POLITICS OF WORLD HUNGER. Copyright © 1973 by Paul and Arthur Simon. All rights reserved. Printed in the United States of America. No part of this book may be used or reproduced in any manner whatsoever without written permission except in the case of brief quotations embodied in critical articles and reviews. For information address Harper & Row, Publishers, Inc., 10 East 53rd Street, New York, N.Y. 10022. Published simultaneously in Canada by Fitzhenry & Whiteside Limited, Toronto.

FIRST EDITION

Designed by Patricia Dunbar

Library of Congress Cataloging in Publication Data

Simon, Paul, 1928–
    The politics of world hunger.
    1. Food supply. 2. Economic development.
3. Economic policy. I. Simon, Arthur, 1930–
joint author. II. Title.
HD9005.S55   338.1'9   72–11589
ISBN 0–06–127776–2

Dedicated to

ELMER GERTZ, a lawyer who has championed the cause of the oppressed; GENE CALLAHAN, a friend who is always willing to help those in need; and NATHAN PAUL SIMON, whose future is apt to be shaped by the way his elders in this country respond to the world's poor.

Contents

We travel together, passengers on a little ship all committed for our safety to its security and peace. We cannot maintain it half fortunate, half miserable; half confident, half despairing; half slave—to the ancient enemies of man—half free in a liberation of resources undreamed of until this day. No craft, no crew can travel safely with such vast contradictions. On their resolution depends the survival of us all.

—ADLAI E. STEVENSON

Although two of us share fully in the authorship of this book, for the sake of style and clarity we use the singular "I" rather than the editorial "we," with Paul as the party of reference when personal experiences are narrated.

—PAUL AND ARTHUR SIMON

Introduction

Paul and Arthur Simon have written a book which is simple in its theme and profound in its conclusions. In a time of apparent retrenchment in U.S. humanitarian commitments, it is an encouraging sign to hear public spokesmen like the Simons call us to a renewed sense of responsibility to our fellow man. The greatest tragedy of our time is that we have apparently lost the capacity to be aware and concerned about the plight of two-thirds of humanity. Those who are concerned about world hunger realize that our destinies in this shrinking globe are inexorably linked in interdependence. This book is an attempt to alert the players in our global scenario to the ominous possibility that we are currently acting out a tragic, nonheroic drama.

We live in a hungry world: a world which hungers for self-determination; a world which hungers for an equitable share of global resources; a world which hungers for food. In the last analysis, no rhetoric can obscure the fact that most of the world's people are hungry, malnourished, and poor. The majority of humanity can no longer be neglected benignly by those who are abundant, well-fed, and wealthy.

The Food and Agriculture Organization of the United Nations recently completed detailed studies of the food-consumption patterns in various areas of the globe. These studies document that, at a "very conservative estimate, some 20 percent of the people in developing countries are undernourished and 60 percent are malnourished." Undernutrition refers to inadequacy in the quantity of food available to an individual. Continued over a long period of time, undernourishment causes loss of weight, disease, and reductions in human energy levels and physical activity. Malnutrition refers to the quality of diet. Nutrients and essential food qualities are needed to enhance a healthy human life. A malnourished person may or may not be undernourished. People who are undernourished are, however, very likely to be malnourished. Both are hungry. The most disturbing element of the report is that in many other developing countries where population has exceeded increases in food production (a situation widespread in the Third World) per capita consumption is less than that of 1939.

Hunger also exists and stubbornly persists in the United States, where resources are abundant. Author Nick Kotz in his challenging book, Let Them Eat Promises, stressed that hunger is a result of unjust distribution of goods, services, and income, and will prevail as long as those systematic evils are ignored. "This nation in the late 1960's looked hunger in the eyes but could not see it." Kotz explains, "We glimpsed at the truth about hunger and called for more study of the problem. . . . This nation should not have needed another survey to know that millions of Americans suffer from inadequate nutrition, not because they are ignorant about proper diet but because they are poor. More than one million Americans live in families with no income at all. Another five million Americans have less total income than the amount the Agriculture Department estimated is needed to maintain a minimum diet. Nine million have such low income levels that maintaining an adequate diet would require from 50 to 100 percent of their available means on food purchases alone. How can these 15 million Americans afford proper nutrition?"

The Politics of World Hunger is a necessary book, because almost nowhere in contemporary America is the quality of people's lives thoroughly debated in public forum. The related issues of poverty and underdevelopment need to be addressed. While the policies of the United States government affect virtually every nation in the world, almost nowhere in this country is the voice of the poor heard on the vital issues and priorities implicit in our foreign policies.

Who speaks for the invisible poor of the world in the United States? Hopefully, organizations like the American Freedom from Hunger Foundation have some effect on the public sphere of opinion in the United States. Programs such as the Walks for Development have initiated local involvement in the needs of the poor. We must remember that only when the issues and concerns affecting the other two billion citizens of the earth become a matter of compassionate concern in the public forum, will action be taken to correct the glaring contradictions of wealth and affluence in the midst of a hungry world.

The Simon brothers suggest that hunger is most properly seen as symptomatic of deeper root causes of world poverty and "underdevelopment." Unless we come to understand the broader context of the literal "politics of world hunger," the plight of the majority of our fellow men and women will remain a mystery forever. The probing concern displayed by the authors for the underlying shibboleths of unemployment, trade barriers, demographic changes, and environmental transformations carry with it deep understanding of the contemporary human condition in a global context.

Ultimately, men and women of good conscience must come to realize that the disparity between the rich and the poor, the haves and the have-nots, the well-fed and the hungry cannot continue. We must face the fact that U.S. foreign policy inherently enhances and sustains this global dichotomy. A democratic tradition like our own cannot long demur on the ethical and political implications of economic systems that exploit, oppress, and chain the poor worker, farmer, and laborer to a way of life that is inconsistent with the precepts of human justice and dignity, as they are so eloquently stated in the United States' Bill of Rights.

The time has come for Americans to rise to the challenge of a worldwide partnership with those who seek to determine their own future development. This is not a military task. This is not a paternalistic burden of the affluent. This is quite properly a task to engage all responsible elements of American society, public and private.

JOHN G. HEALEY
Executive Director
American Freedom from Hunger Foundation, Inc.

A Note to the Reader

Sometimes actors have to exaggerate on stage in order to reach the audience. Frequently writers do the same, hoping they can arouse the public by taking a more strident position on an issue than the facts warrant.

This book does not shout; it does not scream or deal in extremes. It simply discusses things we ignore, and points out the peril of ignoring them. Reality is shocking enough, if the reader reflects on the parade of facts assembled.

The reality to which I refer above all is hungry people. They comprise a majority of the population in most countries of the world, and they go hungry because they are wretchedly poor. There was a time when we could ignore this reality and life for us went on as usual. Not any more. Too many things have put nations in close touch with each other. If conditions become increasingly less tolerable for much of the world, we too will suffer the consequences.

The way we respond to the hungry half of mankind will profoundly influence our foreign policy, our military posture, and even a wide assortment of domestic concerns. Our response is a touchstone of our capacity to make the world livable. This book does not deal with the problem of hunger in a narrow sense, but sees hunger as the starting point for putting other issues into place. The chapters which follow show the relationship of hunger to some of these issues, and suggest major changes.

Inescapably this leads me to propose a grass-roots political movement aimed at revising sharply upward U.S. participation in global economic development. My hope is that those who care about human misery will take part in such a movement, so that we can persuade our leaders to make global development a national goal—and retire from office those who cannot be so persuaded. If political decisions can enable men to get to the moon, political decisions can also enable hungry people to nourish themselves.

Unfortunately the mood of the United States following more than three decades of foreign involvement—some of it wise and some of it foolish—is to forget the rest of the world. After I told David Brown, then executive director of the American Freedom from Hunger Foundation, that this manuscript would soon be published, he wrote me: "The need for fresh material on international development issues has never been as great. . . . The mood of neo-isolation afflicting the country and the strange silence on the part of good candidates is disturbing." Then he noted: *"There is no grass roots constituency for overseas concerns."*

Can such a constituency be mobilized?

Can students who took to the streets to urge U.S. withdrawal from Vietnam become equally concerned about hunger, which kills far more people each day than were killed by our largest bombing raids in Southeast Asia? Was the student protest largely selfish, spurred on because the draft threatened; or was it touched off by a spark of idealism that can also kindle support for impoverished people of the world?

Church groups that reverently, and sometimes proudly, take up an annual collection to help alleviate hunger overseas—are they willing to go one step further and do something far more significant in the political arena?

What about senior citizens, whose potential for rousing interest in world poverty has never been tested? How many hard hats and top hats, liberated and unliberated women, and ordinary people from all walks of life will give the poor of the earth a better chance to struggle for daily bread?

We can find answers to these questions only by challenging people to take part in the cause of international development.

Hunger kills. Because it kills quietly, it does not invite startled attention as does the crack of a rifle or the explosion of a bomb. The sight of a child with a leg shot off shocks us as we see it on our living room television set, but a child with a body exhausted or a mind retarded from lack of nutrition rarely qualifies as news, and even then may not make the same impact. Must hunger and poverty reach the point of explosion before we recognize their enormity?

After seeing the rough draft of this manuscript, a friend wrote: "Most Americans don't really care much about the world. We'd rather not be reminded."

This book directs itself to those who want to face the truth, who dare to be reminded.

PAUL AND ARTHUR SIMON

Part I

HUNGER, POPULATION, AND POVERTY

1

Establishing a Point of View

It could be a game called Reality. Each player starts out with a set of goals that focus on such things as the family, a new house, the church, a job promotion, civic improvement, or retirement plans. Then each draws a major problem—which may or may not appear as an obstacle to those goals. The players must figure out solutions to the problems they have drawn, and afterward the game gadget tells them whether they have helped or hindered their struggle to achieve the chosen goals.

The players are ordinary U.S. citizens working hard to create a better life for themselves and for their children. In doing so, however, they make choices that intersect with a complex set of world conditions.

The first participant, Ronald Wilson—husband, father of three, manager of a hardware store in a small Midwestern town—draws a *problem:* the urban crisis. The parts of the problem are listed: declining tax base for the cities, spiraling costs of maintaining essential services, racial disturbances, crime, unemployment, swelling welfare rolls, and spreading slums. Wilson's *choice:* Let the cities work it out on their own resources. Wilson put in nineteen years to build a house and save a little so that his children can some day go to college. He and his neighbors are law-abiding people, and he believes that hard work and honesty would put the cities back in shape. So, he reasons, the best contribution he can make is to stand up for the virtues that have served him and his townspeople so well. The *outcome:* Wilson's children grow up and move to the city, where they find work. Meanwhile the decay, the costs, and the crime rate there have soared. The younger Wilsons are afraid to walk the streets at night; their children must attend problem-ridden schools; public transportation limps along, while taxes rise. Wilson's children and grandchildren pay for his good intentions with a diminished quality of life. . . .

Next is Mary Viviano, mother, housewife and part-time hair-dresser, who lives in an Eastern city. *Problem:* what to do about "foreign aid." *Choice:* With inflation, rising property taxes, and her husband's income as a salesman uncertain, Mrs. Viviano marks on a questionnaire from her congressman that she favors reducing aid to underdeveloped countries. *Outcome:* Poverty and hunger increase in those countries. They line up more frequently against the United States on international issues, bitter about what they consider to be our callousness. U.S. citizens resent these countries' votes against us in the United Nations and press Congress to cut back economic assistance still more to all but a few friendly nations. Political instability mounts in Latin America, Africa, and Asia. Revolutions and brush-fire wars occur, often with Cold War implications. Since the United States becomes directly involved in several of these, Mrs. Viviano's son is drafted and sent overseas. . . .

Carl Schmidt, a construction worker, lives in a suburb just west of Chicago. The Schmidt family recently moved from the city and is deeply in debt. *Problem:* the Russian military threat. *Choice:* Although Schmidt is highly sensitive about the tax bite on his pay check and on his property, he opts for backing fully the budget recommendations of Pentagon military advisors on the ground that

"You can never be too safe." *Outcome:* The U.S.S.R. matches the United States by stepping up development and production of its own nuclear arsenal. Despite limited agreements, the arms race continues unabated. Increased military spending undercuts efforts to rebuild our cities and clean up the environment. A sense of insecurity deepens for the nuclear powers, and as new weapons are introduced, still more money is drained away from urgent domestic needs. Newscasters bring in mounting reports of links between disease and pollution. Urban areas are particularly neglected, and Schmidt, who is gradually reducing the mortgage on his home, finds that the reduction of the loan coincides with the reduction of property value. . . .

Esther Sovik, a forty-three-year-old widow, supports herself and her daughter by working in a Minneapolis shoe factory. *Problem:* What can be done about persistent unemployment? *Choice:* Conscious of the fact that the firm she works for has a record of diminishing profits, and aware that some shoe factories have already closed because of market losses to foreign imports, Mrs. Sovik favors higher tariffs on imported goods that compete with domestic products. *Outcome:* Congress enacts protectionist legislation. Other countries retaliate by imposing higher tariffs on U.S. products, with consequent damage to this country's export industries. World trade slows and a general global recession begins to take shape. These things adversely affect the entire U.S. economy, increase unemployment, and ultimately force a shutdown of the shoe factory where Mrs. Sovik works. . . .

Elgin Egan, the fifth participant in the game, earns $30,000 a year as a young lawyer for a publishing firm on the West Coast, plus growing returns on stock and real estate investments. *Problems:* poverty abroad and pollution of the U.S. environment. *Choices:* Because Egan takes pride in supporting both antipollution measures and efforts to undo poverty, he decides to contribute to a number of citizen-action groups. *Outcome:* Egan's ostensible choices are wiped out by other, more immediate goals. Egan is a high-powered earner and a high-powered consumer, with just about all his consuming oriented around home and family. Egan's children grow up with inflated appetites for material possessions, and minds conditioned against understanding what it is like to be poor. The cycle that Egan began continues into the next generation, effectively blocking the logical outcome of otherwise sensible views on social issues. His social principles remain abstract while the pursuit of luxuries grabs hold.

Although the five participants differ in many ways, they share one common trait: making decisions on the basis of concerns that are tangible and personally immediate, without adequately considering wider social complications. This prompted them to take actions, the consequences of which undermined their original goals. These players illustrate why we find it so difficult to arrange a livable world.

They also reflect a failure of leadership. Most citizens, occupied with day-to-day demands of job and family, cannot be expected to reach a sufficiently comprehensive understanding of public requirements. That is what leaders are for: to help the public put immediate concerns into the framework of wider obligations and long-range needs. Unfortunately, politics tends to be a short-range enterprise. Elected officials find themselves preoccupied with crises at hand rather than with long-term goals. Put in less flattering words, people seeking office are highly sensitive to voters' likes and dislikes. The surest way to lose an election is to ignore the perceived needs of the electorate. But *perceived* needs, because they are short run and personally immediate, have precisely the fatal characteristic we have noticed of frequently leading to long-range misadventures. This weakness in the democratic process is enlarged to absurdity when candidates for office use scientific polls to find out what the voters want, and adopt the findings as their platform. What the public gets is not leaders, but followers: "yes-men" packaged under the wrong label. When people see their impulses enshrined as policy by respected public figures, they cannot be blamed for cherishing the illusion that those unexamined preferences embody social wisdom.

Can we, before it is too late, arrange human needs in some reasonable order of priority? Can we deal with these needs on that basis? Can we learn to see the world with new eyes?

I propose that we begin at the most fundamental level: man's need for food.

THE HUNGRY WORLD | Far away from us and spread over more than three continents is a world crowded with underfed, ill-fed, and impoverished people who comprise most of the human race. We do not see and hardly understand that strange and distant world, but unless we come to terms with it, we will remain incapable of putting the pieces of the human puzzle together. The five participants in the game of Reality, by operating from a vantage point that did not take this world of misery into account, put their weight inadvertently on the side of a broken future.

Travelers can observe people from this other world. Some of its inhabitants are literally starving to death. I have seen beggars in India, their spindly limbs reaching out for a coin or a piece of bread that might offer the extension of life for a few hours; and I have seen their dead brothers lying in the streets, waiting to be picked up for the only painless journey they ever had. I shall never forget the shock on my first visit to Spain two decades ago: dirty, ragged children, no older than my eight-year-old son, scrambling for orange peelings that a tourist had thrown on a dusty road, and instantly devouring them.

For the most part, however, the hungry of the world are too much a part of the landscape to alarm travelers. They do not beg in the streets and they are not starving to death. But because their bodies and minds have grown accustomed to lack of nourishment since infancy, they are weakened, sometimes mentally retarded, prematurely aged, vulnerable to disease, with opportunities in life—along with life itself—cut short. To work, if possible, and to keep themselves and their families alive consumes all the energy the poorest of the world can muster. Charles H. Weitz, former head of the UN Food and Agriculture Organization's Freedom from Hunger Campaign, gives us an idea of how widespread their predicament is:

> More than 60 percent of the people in the low-income lands are chronically undernourished. Their diets contain about one-third of the protein and two-thirds of the calories considered necessary to maintain health and productivity in an industrialized country. It is the children who suffer the most. In many developing nations half will die from malnutrition during infancy, while more than half the survivors will be physically and mentally stunted for the remainder of their lives.

In short, much of the human race cannot and does not eat well enough "to maintain health and productivity" by our standards, because they are incredibly poor.

Hunger is hidden in the United States, too, and consequently much closer to our doorsteps than we are apt to think. William Turner, his wife, and five children live in East St. Louis, only 15 miles away from my home in Troy, Illinois. With his age, health, and lack of skills against him, Mr. Turner can get only part-time work. Although they are assisted by the state of Illinois, the Turners simply do not have enough purchasing power to eat properly. Furthermore, coming from the rural South to a crowded, neglected urban ghetto, they suddenly encountered a host of living problems that they were not equipped to handle, and these have further diluted their ability to assemble an adequate diet.

Residents of Troy know East St. Louis primarily in terms of crime and decay—understandably, for FBI figures show that East St. Louis ranks repeatedly at or near the top in murders and forcible rape for cities in the nation with a population between 50,000 and 100,000. It gives people in Troy a sense of relief to think that East St. Louis is "not our problem." We do not feel the bite of unemployment as people there do, nor the pain of dependence on welfare, hovels for homes, and running out of groceries a week before the next check comes.

For that matter some people in Troy are too poor to afford a decent diet. I know a few of them, but there are probably others of whom I am not aware, especially among the aged. They are not talking about it, for hunger is something you conceal, if possible. That exposes an irony about hunger in our country: it has become a matter of shame for those who go hungry rather than of shame for us who are well fed.

Appalling and contradictory as hunger is in this productive land, it is dwarfed next to the enormity of world hunger. In the United States the number of hungry people is gradually receding, while on the earth as a whole hunger expands by sheer force of the rate at which the world's population is multiplying. Consequently, despite some impressive gains in the production of food, hunger continues to increase simply because each day brings nearly 200,000 more people to feed. We will soon be adding mouths to the human race at the rate of one billion a decade, more than three-quarters of them to the poor nations.

These nations grow increasingly restless as they see the gap between themselves and the rich nations grow wider and wider. Word has filtered from cities to the most backward rural areas that in the United States and elsewhere, people eat every day until they are full, see physicians when they are sick, and send their children to school. The eyes of the poor have been opened to their own misery, and now they are determined to eat, dress, and dwell in dignity. This is the so-called "revolution of rising expectations," and it may be the most potent force in the world today.

Because rising expectations are often frustrated, they contain seeds of violence. Modernizing efforts in a backward country are no automatic cure either. They may for decades simply tear people from the land and traditions of their fathers, and force them into urban shanties without the work or the wages that put improvement within reach. This situation occurs according to Robert S.

McNamara, President of the World Bank, because uprooted
people pour into the cities before industries are built that might
employ them, and just at the time when industries that do exist are
adapting to laborsaving technology. He adds:

So the cities fill up and urban unemployment steadily grows. Very
probably there is an equal measure of worklessness in the countryside.
The poorest quarter of the population in developing lands risks being
left almost entirely behind in the vast transformation of modern technological society. The "marginal" men, the wretched strugglers for survival on the fringes of farm and city, may already number more than a
half a billion. By 1980 they will surpass a billion. By 1990 two billion.
Can we imagine any human order surviving with so gross a mass of
misery piling up at its base?

In November, 1968, C. P. Snow spoke at Westminster College
in Fulton, Missouri, on the anniversary of the "Iron Curtain"
speech which Winston Churchill gave there in 1945. Addressing
the issue of too many people and not enough food, Lord Snow laid
out his own game of Reality. The world, he said, is approaching a
crisis unlike any other it has ever faced. According to Snow, large-
scale famines will take place, probably after 1980. Before the end
of the century the rich countries will be surrounded by hundreds of
millions of people dying from hunger. We will sit in front of our
television sets and watch them starve to death before our eyes.
Then we will switch our sets off and do nothing. We are already
growing callous about human life, Snow maintains, as a reaction to
the population boom. While we of the rich nations see the world's
poor engulfing us in escalating numbers, we shut ourselves off
from them. Instead of reaching out we are huddling together,
turning inward to protect what we have, behaving as though we
were in a state of siege. Perhaps, he suggests, we will use our
technology to fight off the hungry nations.

What would it take, Snow asks, to prevent this grim scenario?
He lists three things, all of which would have to happen: (1)
involvement of the poor countries in revolutionizing their food

production; (2) an effort by rich and poor countries alike to curtail
or stop the population increase; (3) a joint effort by rich countries,
East and West, to provide food, money, and technical assistance
for the poor. The last, he points out, would require an end to the
armaments race; a kind of cooperation between Russia and the
United States that is without precedent; and sacrifice on the part of
all rich nations "not just in the fairy arithmetic of governments,
but in the ordinary lives of ordinary citizens." Does anyone seriously think this will happen? Of course not, Snow answers.

The picture lends no comfort to those who feel that solutions lie
in planning as usual. Lord Snow may be wrong, of course. I am
hopeful regarding his requirement on food production, for we are
making enough gains to buy a little time. But even if we stave off
the kind of mass starvation which Snow envisions, is there any
reason to believe that a rapidly expanding majority of the world is
going to passively accept hunger and misery as a way of life, while
the wealthy countries—squandering hundreds of billions on a
senseless armaments race—grow wealthier? I think not. Quite
apart from the question of simple justice, by allowing this absurdity to get worse we diminish the possibility that our children, and
children everywhere, will inherit a life of peace.

ONE | For our own and our children's well-being—
HUMAN | to say nothing of the rest of humanity—it is
| essential that we adopt a different world
COMMUNITY | view. This world view does *not* accept our
own surroundings of family, neighborhood, or nation as the
boundaries of concern, to which the rest of the world is appended.
Rather, it sees this entire planet as the one common environment
for all humanity. It looks at the international community as the
setting in which all smaller units of the human race must find a
harmonious place. As a result it is necessary for us to grow beyond
our childhood attachments, and as we once learned that the little
circle of people and places we knew was part of a great nation to

which we belonged, now we must learn that the nation is part of a single, interrelated body of people stretching out and connected to each other around the globe. This is our habitat, and we will make it livable together or we will go down in ruins together.

Not only is this world view totally compatible with love for country, but any lesser view does disservice to our country. This has to be stressed, for as soon as you speak of a sympathy toward the international community which transcends in some important respects the immediate, perceived self-interests of our nation, a kind of knee-jerk patriotism often appears. Rooted in the emotional needs of insecure people, it provides a cause to rally around, but history has shown time and again that instead of true patriotism, it is a mindless, destructive force. The parent who sides with his child no matter how wrong the child may be does not manifest love; on the contrary he uses the child as a tool to shore up his own ego at a vulnerable point, and such a parent inflicts great damage. To say "My country, right or wrong" makes no more sense than to say "My child, right or wrong."

Because the world is one, we cannot separate ourselves from the aspirations of the world's poor. At stake in the outcome of their struggle is also the welfare of our own children and grandchildren, so patriotism needs to be defined in a way which takes this into account. To respond to the hunger dilemma, then, is not to care for one's family or nation less, but to care for humanity more. In the last analysis it is also to care for family and nation more, because it helps them come to terms with the one environment which we share or which destroys us.

Fortunately this world view is becoming more persuasive, because the advance of hunger coincides with other historic developments. Let me name two.

The first is a widespread alarm about the way in which we are polluting and wasting our natural environment. Pollution has been going on for a long time, and prophetic voices have warned us about it; but as recently as 1969 the salvaging of our environment was a cause without a public. Almost overnight it caught on, and today ecology is a familiar word to most high school students. More important, there is a growing awareness that when we deal with the natural environment, we need to care not just for isolated pieces of it, but ultimately to assume a cooperative stewardship for the whole earth—for lands and seas far away from home. It is not just our own sewer system or the county lake or the paper mill up the river that needs attention, since the entire surface of the earth constitutes a unified, interrelated habitat for man. Because we are beginning to see this natural, physical environment as a unit, we can hope for an influence upon our social and political habits—if concern for our natural environment does not *divert* us from tending to the environment of poverty and hunger, a danger I discuss in Chapter 7.

A second development is the exploration of space. Admittedly the race to the moon could prove to be, in retrospect, an outrageous monument to national pride—a $30 billion Superbowl Championship—and in that case it would be profoundly destructive of the world view we are considering. There is another, more hopeful possibility, however, suggested by an experience which both U.S. and Soviet astronauts shared: from "out there" they viewed this tiny globe, unique in our explorable universe in its hospitality to life, as inexpressibly beautiful, precious, and the common inheritance of man. I have rarely been so stirred even at a natural sight as I was when I saw the first colored photograph from the moon of an earth-rise. There it was, this planet earth, over 200,000 miles away, alone and small in the seemingly endless, lifeless expanse of the solar system, a sphere with a thin envelope of elements so carefully balanced as to provide for the drama of human history.

This view of the world urgently needs more adherents, among rank-and-file citizens, because it is in harmony with the physical and moral facts of life, and for that reason it is a vantage point which will enable us to deal sensibly with a variety of problems that confound us. Consider the domestic front. Chronic unemployment, escalating crime, expanding welfare rolls, racial polarization, the spreading of slums, neglect of our rural areas, prisons programmed to turn offenders back onto the streets as hardened criminals, an erosion within both public and private sectors of the will to serve diligently when employed, a loss of confidence in the political process—these, along with the bizarre presence of millions of hungry people in our country, are only some of the impasses. These problems are quite solvable, and our inability to cope effectively with them indicates, as it did with the five game participants, a faulty perspective. It is as though we are lost in a forest at sundown, surrounded by trees that make grotesque, frightening shadows. What we need to do is to see our place in the woods. *A commitment to the entire community of man, one which begins at the point of his need for food, is just the perspective that would enable us to do so.* Solutions will then begin to emerge on some of these internal matters—and with far less anxiety than we now exhibit.

But will we respond to people who hunger? The evidence since the mid-'60s is not encouraging, for during this period U.S. assistance to underdeveloped countries, where the world's hungry are concentrated, steadily shrank.

Why?

First, the war in Vietnam had a draining influence both financially and emotionally. But the reasons for our shrinking response go beyond the war.

A key factor is abdication of leadership at the highest level: presidents without a vision of the world's poor, and senators and congressmen who have their sights fixed on the next election. Following World War II, if your congressman made stirring speeches about feeding hungry people he received cheers—and votes—because when he spoke he was helping Germany, Italy, Great Britain, and other West European nations; and in the audience were people like Carl Schmidt, Mary Viviano, and Ronald Wilson, all with close ties to those countries. Today when your congressman speaks he is more apt to talk about "not pouring foreign aid money down the drain for nations that don't appreciate it." He is aware that the people now assisted live in places like Guatemala or Bangladesh and have no relatives in the audience.

Another reason for failure to respond is ignorance. Although events pour in upon us from every continent and the news media are present, alive and in color, in our living rooms, people tend to pick their news in bits and pieces, smorgasbord style, so that a comprehensive picture is not apt to emerge. Besides, the media fail to cover many issues that are vital to the poor nations. For example, the United Nations Conference on Trade and Development (UNCTAD), an organization of major importance to the poor nations, meets once every four years in order to deal with their development needs. UNCTAD held its last meeting during April and May of 1972 while there was a baseball strike in the United States. The media probably devoted 1,000 times more ink and television time to that strike than to the voice of the underdeveloped world. Most of us knew about the baseball strike. But who heard of UNCTAD?

Related to ignorance is remoteness. Television helps us to see hungry people, but immediate replay of dislocated refugees, napalmed children, or starving Pakistanis also has an impersonal quality to it; it is not *really* happening (we have seen too many movies), or it is happening far away to strange people we do not know and whose lives do not touch our own. Bracketing these snatches of news are messages telling us to spend money on a host of attractions—one offers a choice of eight different meat combinations for my dog—so the total effect, far from orienting our thinking and behavior around a concern for these desperate people, may brainwash us against such a response.

A feeling of helplessness also lingers with many of us. Hunger and the problems surrounding it appear so enormous, so overwhelming that we are apt to wring our hands and despair of doing anything at all. If a person believes he "can't fight city hall" in his own community, in a culture which he more or less understands, how can he possibly make a dent on an international dilemma of seemingly infinite size and complexity? The will to help may be present, but the means of doing so escape us.

Undisguised apathy, too, accounts for our diminishing response. Selfishness is an enduring part of human nature, and in the end people may simply believe what they want to believe about the world, and do what they prefer to do. It may be possible to shock a few complacent souls into a state of good sense by appealing to their long-range self-interest, or to hope for mental or moral conversion, but the grip of apathy is hard to break.

Barriers such as these between ourselves and the hungry world account for widespread assumptions, shared by too many elected officials, that U.S. citizens in general and blue collar workers in particular

cannot face their shortcomings,

want to perpetuate economic and racial division in the world,

and

will listen only to easy simplistic solutions.

Candidates reinforce those assumptions when they obtain public office by pandering to our least generous instincts. One of the most discouraging aspects of U.S. political life is the tendency to nominate and elect those who corrupt the truth for the sake of political convenience, who tell the crowds what they want to hear rather than what they should hear. Instead of being challenged to assume responsibility for improving the world, the nation is turned inward. That may be "good politics," but it leads to ruinous policies.

There is a more hopeful side, however. Growing numbers of people have an uneasy suspicion that the patchwork of painless reforms and improvements usually proposed by candidates for public office does not come to grips with the social crisis here at home, much less in the world. These citizens want honest solutions, not political babyfood. In my travels throughout Illinois, meeting with hundreds of civic clubs, farm organizations, churches, and other groups, I sense that despite the weaknesses that hold each of us back, most people would like to befriend their fellow human beings. They do not want to be taken for suckers or pour money into the bulging pockets of some merchant or corrupt official overseas. The idea of one world may be a little abstract, but hungry people still have some flesh-and-blood reality for them. In short, I think people are willing to sacrifice in order to build a better life for their children and for the children of the world, *if they can be shown the way.*

Sanity calls for a candid discussion of issues in order to convince the average citizen that his actions can help to change the world.

People can do something. A feeling of helplessness is a self-fulfilling prophecy, but simple, concrete actions can exert an important influence toward feeding the hungry and establishing a better, more peaceful world. These actions include the work of private organizations; but they also, and most urgently, require us to take part in political affairs so that national priorities reflect the best and not the worst in us. For fiscal year 1973 we will spend more than $100 per person for financing the federal indebtedness (largely because of political cowardice; indebtedness is politically easier than taxation or cutting expenditures), 17 times as much as we will provide for economic assistance to the poor abroad. Is there sufficient reason, for example, why we have to spend $375 a year per citizen for current military purposes and $6 a year per citizen on economic assistance to impoverished countries? If enough people can be persuaded to revive the conscience of our lawmakers on economic assistance—and back this up with door-to-door work before elections—we will witness a quick movement away from such folly. A great deal depends on whether or not people who are accustomed to answering human needs on a personal basis or through charitable agencies will be able to shift gears and translate their convictions into political decisions as well.

But it must be done soon.

United States withdrawal from Vietnam imposes on the nation a moment of truth that has profound consequences for the entire world. What will characterize our stance toward the rest of mankind? Nuclear overkill and a global military presence? Retreat from problems beyond our borders? Or participation with the poor nations in developing a livable world? A great many of us have come to deplore this country's role in Vietnam. Can we now, by some contorted logic, believe that it is wrong to pour bombs on innocent people, but permissible to let a thousand times as many go hungry and die through neglect? If so, history will certainly judge the latter to have been a far greater violence against humanity.

2

The Hungry Majority

The baby's stomach bulged. His arms and legs looked like sticks, and although four and a half months old, Jesus Sanchez weighed no more than he did at birth. The diagnosis: calorie starvation, scurvy, rickets, pneumonia, and no detectable vitamin C in his blood.

Guatemala? Peru? No, Southwestern U.S.A., 1971. H. Peter Chase, a Colorado pediatrician, was presenting medical statistics to the Senate Committee on Nutrition when his slide projector flashed the picture of little Jesus on the wall. A hush came over the gallery as Dr. Chase continued his report, for hunger had suddenly turned from a dull record into a visible tragedy.

As the child of migrant workers, Jesus belongs to a group that Edward R. Murrow described in a 1960 CBS documentary, "Harvest of Shame." On that broadcast one of the farmers said, "We used to own our slaves. Now we just rent 'em." Ten years later an NBC documentary, "Migrant," showed that slaves are still being rented. In 1971 migrant workers averaged an annual income of $1,400. They rank among the worst housed, least protected by law, and least educated people in the United States. Their families are also among the most hungry.

They are not alone. Probably a majority of the 26 million people in our country living below the poverty line—two-thirds of them white—is still poorly nourished. Few reach an advanced stage of starvation, but many of them are physically or emotionally damaged. Since malnourishment often leads to mental retardation, it is no accident that three-fourths of the nation's mentally retarded come from areas of urban and rural poverty.

One family my brother visited tries to eke out a living on 20 acres of land. The health of both parents is failing. Without government food commodities the family could not survive, although it still means a diet of bread and beans the last ten days of each month. Five of the seven children attend school, where they watch while the other children eat, because the half price of 15 cents a lunch—$3.75 a week for five—is more than the family can afford.

We have made notable gains against hunger during the past five years, but government food programs still do not reach millions of the most needy, nor are the programs sufficient for all who participate. Yet in 1972 the Administration returned $688 million to the U.S. Treasury that Congress had appropriated for food programs. The past two administrations offered glowing promises about wiping out hunger, but hedged and dragged their feet repeatedly on concrete measures. Without the pressure of embarrassment from public hearings and special reports by the news media, gains of the past five years would not have taken place. Even so, our food stamp program cost the federal treasury $1.8 billion in 1972 —an amount less than the government gives in tax-loophole subsidies to the nation's 3,000 families with annual incomes of more than a million dollars.

How can we estimate the extent of hunger in our country? The number of people below the poverty line gives one indication. Studies show that even the *least* poor of the poor can barely afford an economy diet carefully worked out by the U.S. Department of Agriculture. The government estimates that among those who follow this Economy Plan diet, only one family in ten can nourish itself adequately. The Bureau of Budget backs this up: "The Economy Plan is an emergency diet intended to be used during periods of temporary economic distress. As a permanent diet, the Economy Plan fails to provide sufficient caloric value although minimum levels of other essential nutrients are sustained." One reason the economy diet does not work is that it assumes sophisticated planning abilities, refrigeration, transportation, and bulk purchases— things that low-income families often lack. Consequently it is safe to say that 11 million U.S. citizens below the poverty line and without food assistance cannot eat what they need. To these add millions more whom food assistance helps, but not enough, and countless others who rise above the statistical poverty line, but cannot afford an adequate diet.

Mrs. Lucille Knox of Chicago and her three children receive $3,775 in public assistance, well below the poverty line. Food stamps increase their allowance by $38 a month. In theory the family can afford the government's economy diet, but in fact other expenses deprive them of that. For example, assistance to the Knox family includes a rent ceiling of $97 a month that applies to welfare families in Chicago, but the Knoxes have to pay $130. The difference comes out of their food money. When emergencies strike—and the poor are particularly vulnerable to them—money cannot be taken from fixed expenses, so the Knox children learn to eat less. Yet partly because of the stigma attached to poverty, roughly one-third of Chicago's families below the poverty line has not even applied for assistance.

Decatur, soybean capital of America, and a major processor of Illinois's grain, had an unemployment rate of 5 percent in 1972. Nearly two thousand Decatur families had incomes below the poverty line that year. That means a lot of hungry people.

My brother Art is a Lutheran minister in Manhattan's Lower

East Side, one of New York's most crowded slums. A few years ago a nutritional study of six primary schools in his neighborhood tested 619 children. The diets of almost three-fourths were rated poor, which meant they got half or less than half of their daily requirement of vitamins. One out of six had a clinical rating of poor—which showed up in such things as excessive leanness and prominent abdomens. Art says that about one-fourth of the youngsters who attend public elementary school across the street from his apartment fail to eat breakfast—a school in which the reading level of 90 percent of the children fell below the national average in 1972. Obviously hunger there is contributing to learning retardation among children who need every bit of help they can get, without which many can only grow up accumulating problems that even in purely economic terms will prove costly to us.

These illustrations from Illinois and New York are relatively "happy" ones since both states help the poor much more than most states do. A family of four on public aid in New York gets five times as much as the same family in Mississippi. As a nation, we have yet to take the sensible stand that the state of a person's need determines the help he receives, not the state of his residence.

The fact that the richest nation on earth has within itself a sizable "underdeveloped country" of poor and hungry people does no particular honor to us. Not another wealthy, industrialized nation, East or West, tolerates the kind of slums, the persistent unemployment, the lack of medical coverage, or the hunger that still characterize the United States. Japan, for example, has wiped out hunger. All Japanese school children are furnished scientifically balanced lunches with nutrients added. Pregnant mothers and young children get special attention, with a food-supplement program available to all mothers during and after pregnancy. Instead of being relief-oriented, Japan's feeding programs are considered a fundamental investment in the nation. In 1971 citizens of Kobe, Japan, sent a gift of food to Seattle's unemployed Boeing workers, who struggled unsuccessfully for five months to get food assistance from our government.

Most observers believe that even China, despite its poverty, has eliminated hunger. But not the United States.

It would be a relatively simple matter to end hunger within our borders. First, we could adopt a policy of guaranteed employment, with the government acting as employer of last resort. If every employable head of family had a job that paid a wage by which he or she could sustain the family above the poverty level, millions of poorly fed citizens would begin to eat well. Second, it is indefensible to punish children, old people, and handicapped people. So those who cannot or should not work also need to receive an income that lifts them above poverty. Marginal cases—those unwilling to work, for example—could be dealt with separately, and food commodities made available for emergencies.

Why, then, with our wealth, has widespread hunger been permitted to exist in the United States? Part of the answer lies in a long history of devotion to a particular understanding of free enterprise that exalts financial success, while branding the destitute as moral delinquents. It is a viewpoint that at an earlier period wanted no government restraints on giant monopolies, but at the same time demanded that authorities act to outlaw and forceably repress the rise of organized labor—all in the name of free enterprise.

The idea that poverty is the result of moral failure is sufficiently widespread that over the years outrageous contradictions have developed. For example, most of the overseas and domestic food-assistance programs were started for the purpose of bolstering U.S. farm incomes, not to reduce or eliminate hunger. Today huge federal subsidies are paid to wealthy farm operators (small farmers receive much less), while only a pittance, by comparison, goes to poverty-stricken people for food assistance. Congressman Jamie Whitten, Chairman of the powerful House Agricultural Appropriations Subcommittee, represents a Mississippi district that according to the 1970 census had 144,952 people below the poverty line—a full third of its population. Most poor families there earned well under $2,000 that year. In fiscal year 1971, more than a thousand large producers in Whitten's district received $28 million in farm subsidies, while the poor people there got $17 million for food assistance. The large producers averaged $26,667 each, poor people $116. Actually those who received food assistance averaged nearly twice that much, because almost half of the poor people in Whitten's district got no food assistance at all.

The same year Senator James Eastland's family in Sunflower County, Mississippi, received federal subsidies of $164,000. (Because a congressional law limited some types of subsidies to $55,000, the Eastlands created several business entities to farm their cotton plantation.) Five hundred and seventy wealthy farmers in Sunflower County were given a total of more than $10 million in government handouts in fiscal year 1971, while 20,000 poor people—over half of the county's population—got only $2.3 million in food assistance.

These figures illustrate a monstrous irrationality: giant handouts to the rich for keeping farmland idle, while millions go hungry. Yet this only begins to show how government policy has subsidized the wealthy and driven poor farmers and farm workers off the land, often leaving them to waste away nearby or in a distant urban slum, in this way piling up for the nation a huge debt in physical and emotional outcasts.

Hungry people are sucked into the vortex of other problems. An example is Cairo at the southern tip of Illinois, an economically depressed town and one of the most racially polarized communities in the nation. For more than three years Cairo's blacks have boycotted white businesses. Shoot-outs, killings, bombings, and fires occur periodically, but meaningful negotiation has not taken place. The Rev. Jesse Jackson, head of Operation PUSH, made this perceptive observation:

We see racial tension on the surface in Cairo. But beneath the surface, the basic problem is hunger. . . . There are more people than jobs and a seasonal welfare system that cannot meet the needs of all the people. Poor whites and poor blacks, blinded by their hunger, cannot see that the real need is to eliminate poverty, not each other.

Serious as hunger still is for many of our citizens, it cannot be compared either in extent or intensity to hunger for most of the world's poor. The experience of hunger here does, however, underscore some lessons that can be applied even in underdeveloped countries. One is that while feeding hungry people is costly, failure to do so is much more expensive in the long run, because the wreckage of human lives has to be paid for many times over in other ways. Hungry people mean economic stagnation. Another lesson is that advanced technology and high food production do not in themselves wipe out hunger. *Where people are mired in poverty, there you will find hunger, thriving right along with a food-surplus problem.* Therefore the most fundamental and difficult part of the hunger question has to do with remedying the worst features of economic inequality.

WHAT IS IT LIKE TO BE HUNGRY? Albert van den Heuvel of the World Council of Churches speaks about the latter days of World War II in his native Holland:

During the winter of 1944–45 I was hungry. We lived on a bowl of soup and one piece of bread a day. One day my mother had some pies and made me take one to my grandmother. I ate it all on the way, and told my parents that I had been attacked on the road. I loved my grandmother, but hunger is stronger than love.

Van den Heuvel recalls a distinguished professor of law coming to his door begging for potato peels; and a couple arrested for having eaten part of their child who had starved to death. The couple broke down with remorse not after the charges against them were dropped, but after they had been fed by the police.

Hunger is a horrible companion, but few of the world's hungry ever live and flourish to tell the world what it is like. They just quietly suffer and die, victims not so much of stomach pains as of weakness, apathy, retardation, and disease caused by deficient diets.

In *Living Poor,* Moritz Thomsen, a forty-eight-year-old farmer, reports his years as a Peace Corps worker in a remote tropical village of Ecuador. There he discovered what it means that most of the world's farmers are able to work only three or four hours a day. The villagers' laziness initially outraged Thomsen. But when he was forced by circumstances to eat what they ate, he, too, became "lazy" and often wound up sick in bed—even though his body was not debilitated, like everyone else's, with crawling worms. "There is only so much energy in a dish of rice and a piece of fish," writes Thomsen. "There are just so many miles to a gallon of bananas—not one foot more."[1] Thomsen, who paid a village family to let him eat his evening meal with them, describes the pathetic sight of their baby girl, malnourished and sickly, sleeping on the floor during mealtimes, or eating bits of banana or rice off the floor. He received favored treatment as a paying guest, but even that became more meager:

Instead of fish and rice, we were tucking away *aba* soup, and rice with *abas, abas* being a large, fat tasteless bean about 200 percent blander than a lima bean. The evening meal became more and more spiritual. A dozen or so times I staggered over to Alexandro's house, ravenous with hunger and anticipation, to find that supper was one well-centered and naked fried egg cowering on the plate. What made even this more or less tasteless was my knowledge that it was the only egg in the house and that the rest of the family was supping on cups of hot water and brown sugar and platano, an enormous, banana-like monstrosity, about 99 percent starch, which was as tasteless as paper. Eating the only egg in the house while the youngest child slowly wasted away from malnutrition didn't help things either.

During a drought, Thomsen reports, people in a nearby village "were selling their children before they died of hunger; autopsies on the ones who had died revealed stomachs full of roots and dirt." In his own village, the birth of a stillborn child was occasion for jubilant celebration, since it meant that someone had become an *angelito* without all the intervening suffering.

These are the feelings of hunger.

HOW WIDESPREAD IS HUNGER? Imagine ten children at a table dividing up food. The three healthiest load their plates with large portions, including most of the meat, fish, milk, and eggs. They eat what they want and discard the leftovers. Two other children, through heroic efforts, barely get enough to meet their basic requirements. The remaining five are left wanting. Three or four of them—sickly, nervous, and apathetic children—manage to stave off hunger pains by eating too many starch foods. Another one or two who cannot even do that eventually will perish from some disease such as diarrhea or pneumonia which they are too weak to ward off. Obviously such a family would have a great many problems besides hunger to contend with, and so it is in the human family, of which these children are a parable.

The Food and Agriculture Organization of the United Nations estimates that one-third to one-half of the world's people suffer from nutritional deprivation. In the low-income countries alone, one-half to two-thirds fall into that category by various estimates. Norman E. Borlaug, who has played a key role in expanding world food production, estimates that half of the world's population is undernourished and two-thirds is malnourished. It is fair to conclude that in poor countries as a whole, the poor comprise a hungry majority.

We call nutritionally deprived people "hungry," even though the term is far from precise and may or may not include the *feeling* of hunger. Some are *under*nourished—incapable of getting enough calories each day to provide their bodies with fuel for minimal demands. These calorie-deficient persons number about a half billion, and the total would rise substantially if it were figured on the basis of people's potential (rather than minimal) functioning capacity. Others—perhaps half the world's population—are *mal*nourished. They get their calories, but the quality is seriously defective. These people are primarily protein-deficient.

A protein gap, therefore, causes most of the hunger, and unfortunately the gap is widening. According to Paul E. Johnson,

Operations Division Chief of Food for Peace, protein in the diets of people in high-income countries has increased since World War II by 6 percent, while in low-income countries protein has *decreased* by approximately the same percentage. Addeke H. Boerma, Director-General of the FAO, says that two-thirds of the world's preschool children suffer enough malnutrition to retard their physical growth and permanently damage their health. We have known for a long time that protein deficiency stunts physical growth and causes or provides occasion for disease. But in recent years a sinister twist has been added with mounting evidence that it can also cause permanent mental retardation, especially during prenatal development and during the first three or four years of life. Since more than 80 percent of the world's births take place in low-income countries, we are clearly talking about a huge stake in the future. The U.S. Committee for UNICEF states the problem this way:

> Every half minute, 100 children are born in developing countries. Twenty of them will die within the year. Of the 80 who survive, 60 will have no access to modern medical care during their childhood. An equal number will suffer from malnutrition during their crucial early years, with the possibility of irreversible physical and mental damage.

In addition to calorie deficiency and protein deficiency (or shortage of other nutrients), there is a third and still more obstinate dimension to hunger: "income deficiency." The persistence of *poverty* above all frustrates otherwise achievable means of getting people above the hunger line. Some of poverty's stubbornness stems from the population explosion, for if within a few decades we had the population problem basically in hand, and made peace with our environment, we could almost certainly develop the necessary food-producing technology to feed the world. But there are two catches to that possibility. First, as I argue in the next chapter, poverty itself virtually guarantees an unmanageable growth rate in population. Second, even if food-producing technologies somehow catch up and keep pace with the population, but

billions of people remain so poor that they cannot purchase the
food produced, hunger will grind on mercilessly. /

THE GREEN | In 1941 three agricultural scientists and one
REVOLUTION | graduate student traveled the dirt roads of
Mexico to learn all they could about farming
in that country. What they saw depressed them: peasants struggling to coax a stingy harvest out of the earth. Their report
prompted the establishment in 1943 of a research center in Mexico
to develop strains of corn, wheat, and beans that could increase the
nation's food supply. Not only has Mexico multiplied its production of these crops since then, but in the mid-1960s a number of
Asian countries introduced "Mexican dwarf wheat" with impressive results. These gains, along with the development of high-yield
strains of rice in the Philippines, gave birth to the "green revolution." By 1971, 50 million acres—more than half of these in
India—had been planted in new strains of wheat and rice.

But has a green revolution taken place? Not according to
Boerma: "Over the entire decade of the 1960s the trend of food
production per head showed virtually no increase in any of the
developing regions, and actually fell behind somewhat in Africa."
This trend continued in 1970. In 1971 per capita food production
fell almost 1 percent in those regions, and preliminary reports for
1972 showed serious setbacks in grain production in Asia. /What
has occurred, however, are overall advances in the production of
wheat and rice (and to a lesser extent some other grains) since
the mid-1960s, probably large enough to stave off massive famines
widely predicted for the 1970s. /

/But the green revolution "does not yet have enough of the
general economic and social thrust behind it which we have all
along said would be necessary and without which it will fail in its
broader objectives for bettering standards of life in the developing
countries," in the opinion of Boerma. /

Until recently most underdeveloped countries have managed to keep per capita food production from falling by putting extensive pasture and forest lands under the plow. But the amount of new land suitable for cultivation without massive investment is rapidly running out. Most additional food will have to come from higher production on already cultivated land, more and more of which is being lost to sprawling cities and industries. In short, the "green revolution" *has* to spread, or even the most cautious hopes for improvement will be shattered.

Assuming the best in terms of production increases, high-yield varieties still illustrate the underlying dilemma: *Can the benefits of improved production reach the hungriest people, or will they stay with the already well-fed and simply widen the gap between the poor and the prosperous?* That question pushes these hard knots to the surface:

1. Per capita production increases tell us about an average, but they do not indicate how the extra food and earnings are distributed. Maldistribution has been the most intractable shortcoming in most poor countries. (Remember the statistician who waded across a stream three feet deep on the average, and drowned.)

2. So far the main advantages have gone to those farmers who are relatively prosperous. The Rockefeller Foundation, a principal sponsor of the research institutes that developed the "miracle seeds," quite candidly reports: "Large-scale programs designed to remedy massive national food deficits are necessarily geared to the farmer who can afford some investment in seed, fertilizer and machinery." Irrigation, pesticides, and roads may also be required costs, and unless poverty-stricken farmers are trained in the needed skills and offered credit on fair terms, they can easily be ruined. Many already have been.

3. The "green revolution" could provide millions of new jobs, as well as additional income for the rural poor. But if machines replace men, or if cereal prices fall because markets do not open for this harvest, many farmers will be driven off the land or back to subsistence farming.

4. Farmers in low-rainfall areas, where irrigation is not avail-

The Hungry Majority 31

able and where neither new seeds nor multiple cropping are feasible, are also likely to be adversely affected by the improved competitive position of others, unless they are helped toward more productive methods. The FAO says that on *two-thirds* of the cultivated land in underdeveloped countries the high-yielding seeds cannot be used.

These are not the only problems that threaten hopes attached to the surge in cereal production. Blights gave the Philippines major reversals in 1971 and 1972, forcing that country to import large quantities of rice once more. Nor do the new varieties answer the more pervasive problem of protein deficiencies. Wheat is relatively low in protein, rice even more so—and over half of the world's population gets 80 percent of its calories from rice. In addition, the population explosion will continue to devour most of the production gains, although some valuable years have been secured for fending off that hungry giant.

All these obstacles underscore the fundamental importance of political decisions and social reforms that are necessary to let people work their way out of poverty. A few years ago Eugene R. Black, then Chairman of the Overseas Development Council, posed the issue well, despite a touch of undue optimism:

Skillfully handled in the 'seventies the Green Revolution can become the vehicle for eliminating most of the malnutrition and hunger that now cripples half of the people of this planet and for providing millions of new jobs in the countryside. Poorly managed, the new seeds and their associated technologies could displace millions in the countryside, forcing them to the already overcrowded cities.

The technology is on the way. But how will it be used? And who will reap the harvest?

ASIA | Asia contains about one-quarter of the world's tilled land. Asians consume about one-quarter of the world's food. Yet more than half of the world lives in Asia.

It requires seven Asian farmers to produce enough to supply

their own families plus three nonfarm families, and that on a badly deficient level. By contrast, one U.S. farmer produces enough to sustain 19 nonfarm families. In order to support the number of nonfarm families that our single U.S. farmer supports, it would take *forty-four* Asian farmers. Furthermore, since rural Asia is caught so completely in the upward population spiral, the rate of production per farmer has been falling rather than rising. One study shows that over a 50-year period ending in 1964, while the number of Asians employed in agriculture doubled, their average productivity per farmer fell by about 20 percent.

These figures indicate the extent to which Asia depends on the "green revolution." All the more so in view of an FAO estimate (which does not include communist countries) that by 1985 "practically the entire *potential* arable area will be under the plough" in that region. With the prospect of hundreds of millions of additional Asians soon living on farms, and acreage suitable for new cultivation closing out, existing farmland has to become more productive and labor-intensive. In addition, if subsistence-level farmers cannot take part in improved methods, especially those connected with high-yield cereals, they will be driven off the land in even greater hordes and become part of unimaginable human cesspools in the cities. In that case higher production might *increase* the number of hungry people.

India illustrates this dilemma well.

A poor tenant farmer in India cultivates several acres in one or more patches. He works with primitive tools, such as a hoe or a wooden plow. He scavenges manure not for fertilizer but for fuel. Without irrigation he depends entirely on the rains for a harvest. When the harvest comes, half goes to the landlord, some is stored for food, some for seed, some pays off debts, and whatever remains is sold to a middleman—who may also be landlord and loan shark—at an excessively low price. On that bit of cash the farmer's family depends for additional food and whatever else it may need for an entire year: a few pieces of cloth, medicine, and occasional transportation. If the farmer has three sons and one of them moves to the city to join the urban unemployed, the man's few acres still have to be divided between the remaining sons. In this way farm holdings become smaller and smaller as the population rises. But at some point even hungry subsistence is no longer possible, and the farmer or his sons will die or move on, with the acres going to a more prosperous tenant who can invest in better methods of production. For that matter, even if the farm is not fragmented, competition from higher cereal yields elsewhere could drive the farmer's income down, and that might still wipe him out.

This kind of situation has its counterpart in the United States, to be sure, but with the striking difference of India's overall poverty. In mid-1972 almost half of that country's farm families owned an acre of land or less—and "less" for almost half of them meant owning no land at all. Per capita income in India averages about $90 a year. More important, the bottom 200 million, a population roughly that of the United States, has an annual per capita income of about $35, or 10 cents a day. Even if India's present five-year plan achieves its goals, by 1974 these people will earn an average of 12 cents a day. On another scale, an Indian government survey showed in 1970 a per capita consumption of less than 18 cents a day by 289 million of its people—more than half the population. Ten years earlier, only 184 million Indians lived below that level. The increase of extremely poor Indians thus matched India's total increase in population for the same decade, indicating where its more than one million additional people each month seem destined to go.

Not surprisingly, this has an adverse effect on food consumption in India. *The New York Times* reported in 1971 that, partly because of the population spiral and rising food prices, "the average infant receives 8 percent less protein than did one born in 1960." And this is a country where, by government estimates, 80 percent of its children suffer from "malnutritional dwarfism," principally caused by protein deficiency, and where at least 10,000 children go blind each year from lack of vitamin A.

The above limitations need to be kept in mind when we assess the positive gains of the "green revolution" in India, where it has most widely taken hold. The new high-yield cereal varieties address primarily the problem of calorie hunger, not the more widespread problem of protein hunger. In addition, when the government of India speaks of reaching self-sufficiency in grain production, and even of exporting rice and wheat, it speaks in terms dictated by the necessity of earning foreign currency in order to pay for other essential imports, but not in terms of raising nutritional levels.

India is virtually a vegetarian nation, with animal products constituting perhaps 3 percent of the food it consumes. Although India has one-third of the world's cattle, its widespread taboo on animal slaughter eliminates one major potential source of protein. More significant, the cattle themselves are victims of hunger and therefore provide little milk and little work—weak oxen cannot plow well or haul heavy loads. The average annual yield of milk per cow in India is 58 gallons, compared to 1,144 gallons per cow in Israel.

Gunnar Myrdal has laid great stress on internal social obstacles that prevent India (and many other impoverished countries) from raising the general standard of living. The caste system, fatalism, socially inert religion, and hundreds of local languages are among things deeply ingrained that fall into this category. They stand as formidable hindrances to feeding hungry people.

In much of Asia the situation is roughly comparable to that in India, with some countries faring better. Bangladesh ranks well below India, with an average per capita income by some estimates of $30 a year even before the upheavals of 1971. Pakistan's per capita earnings surpass India's, an interesting index, since a medical study in 1970 of a Pakistani community near Lahore found that 87 percent of the infants failed to get sufficient food before they completed their first year of life. Many of the mothers were themselves too poorly fed to nurse their infants adequately, and the study found that "it takes about one-third to one-half of the basic family income to feed an infant under five months with adequate quantities of milk."

The Japanese eat far better than any other Asian people, a reflection of advanced industrialization and a high standard of living. Japan's farms are small and cultivated so intensively that observers have called it "horticulture" rather than agriculture. Despite Japan's ingenuity in food production, including global fishing activities, Japan still has to import great quantities of food, and most of Japan's proteins come from rice, soybeans, and other crops. For a half century Japan engaged in forceable expansion, a fact which can be attributed in part at least to population pressures and the need for enlarging food supplies. Japan now makes a valuable contribution to international peace, but serious economic difficulty, such as a setback in world trade, could place Japan in a volatile situation.

China has apparently moved itself out of the "hungry" category through rigorously imposed sharing of poverty, although information about that country is still limited. Food is carefully, even severely rationed, but all peasants are assured a minimally acceptable diet, which places many of them far ahead of anything they previously knew. Prior to the "ping-pong diplomacy," which opened the door for U.S. citizens and other Western observers, hunger had been considered widespread in China. That suspicion was no doubt well founded earlier. U.S. observers who entered, starting in 1971, were uniformly impressed, however, with the strides that had been made. "Hordes of beggars and of the starving and diseased that once were familiar are gone. The people look healthy and are obviously adequately fed," reported Seymour Topping of *The New York Times*. Edgar Snow wrote of the Chinese peasant: "Our man is well fed, healthy, adequately clad, fully employed. . . . He lives within a very narrow budget but he is free from bank mortgages, debt and fear of starvation and beggary which plagued his parents."

AFRICA | During the 1960s food production gains in Africa failed to keep pace with population growth. According to FAO, more Africans are turning to rodents, insects, caterpillars, maggots, and snails for their protein supply—not by choice but by necessity.

Why this movement backward? A harsh natural environment and subsistence-level poverty characterize much of Africa and impose hostile conditions on efforts to reduce hunger, or even hold it in line. The Sahara Desert consumes one-third of Africa and is growing. (In 1971 Algeria and Upper Volta appealed for international help in halting the desert's annual advance over farmland.) Much of the rest of Africa is tropical, with soil that cannot be cultivated along traditional Western lines because it hardens when exposed to the sun. Jungles, disabling heat, and dangerous pests such as parasitic worms and tsetse flies make farming in the tropics a difficult enterprise.

Measured in terms of income, most of Africa falls below an average of $100 a year per person. Nigeria, the continent's most populated nation, with 58 million people, has a per capita annual income of about $80, an illiteracy rate of 85 percent, over 200 languages or dialects, and most of its people are poorly nourished. Still, with one-sixth of Africa's population, Nigeria is often cited as the nation that must lead the way on that continent.

Only a few African countries achieve a per capita income above $300 a year. Libya and South Africa rank highest, and in each case the figures obscure the fact that a tiny minority controls the wealth, while the masses distribute poverty among themselves. Libya's money comes from oil. In South Africa four million whites own 87 percent of the land, and 16 million nonwhites occupy the rest. The *Times* of London published a study in 1971 showing South Africa's whites with a per capita yearly income over $2,400, compared to $127 for Africans, but even the latter figure hides a huge disparity between city and rural workers. Black and colored city workers earn much more than those on subsistence agriculture in the rural black settlements. Not that blacks escape poverty in the cities. A few years ago the National Nutrition Research Institute in Pretoria reported that 80 percent of the African school children in Pretoria came from homes too poor to prevent malnutrition, and calculated the yearly incidence in South Africa of marasmus (a calorie-starvation disease) and kwashiorkor (a protein-starvation disease) to be 29,000 and 36,000 respectively.

Southwest Africa, Rhodesia, and the Portuguese colonies of Angola, Mozambique, and Portuguese Guinea also have an elite white minority dominating impoverished Africans.

While those situations are no longer typical of Africa, poverty and hunger are. Much of the cultivated land in Africa grows "cash crops" such as cocoa, coffee, nuts, and cotton, which are sold abroad for foreign exchange, and without which countries cannot purchase essential imports. But not enough skilled farming helps feed hungry Africans, who rely mainly on their own primitive agriculture to stay alive. Women often work with crude hand tools, growing mainly starchy roots, while men seek employment on plantations or in industries away from home, or may fish and hunt. Most Africans scratch out a living in ways that seem certain to reward them with inadequate diets and poor health.

What are the prospects for improvement?

According to the Food and Agriculture Organization, Africa north of the Sahara can sharply increase its production of cereals by using high-yield varieties. FAO says that in much of North Africa over half of the arable land lies fallow every year, but that where rainfall is adequate, the fallow could be cropped with pulses (peas, beans, lentils) or leguminous fodder crops for livestock. In the long run, if an inexpensive method of converting salt water to fresh water is developed, or if water can be "mined" from the earth's crust beneath the Sahara Desert, the outlook for North Africa would improve sharply.

Egypt's Aswan Dam provides North Africa's most dramatic example of an assault on hunger. The dam has brought its share of reverses, however, including loss of fertility on land previously flooded each year by the Nile. Ultimately Egypt hopes for two million additional acres of farmland from this project, two-thirds from the desert. At the 1971 dedication, Egypt's Minister of Electric Power said that 650,000 acres had already been reclaimed from the desert, but he also conceded that during the eleven years of work on the project, population growth of about eight million more Egyptians had outstripped the country's ability to expand cropland. In this respect the project does little more than buy time.

South of the Sahara hardly any land is suitable for the new high-yield cereals, with the Malagasy Republic the most notable exception. Tropical Africa does have huge reserves of uncultivated land, but its use remains a long-range process requiring jungle clearance, malaria and tsetse-fly control, and population resettlement, all tedious and costly. In addition intensive research is needed to develop the neglected science of tropical agriculture. Increasing protein in cassava and other starchy roots is an early goal, and even that may take years. The International Institute of Tropical Agriculture in Ibadan, Nigeria, opened in 1970, will help to link other research centers for tropical agriculture into a small network. But research is minuscule in proportion to Africa's need.

LATIN AMERICA | Latin American should be much better off than Asia and Africa. It has a markedly higher per capita output, is more industrially developed, and its ratio of cultivated land per person is greater. Yet the Rockefeller Report in 1969 estimated that food production per person fell 10 percent in Latin America since the end of World War II. Why? Along with population growth an underlying factor is the gap between rich and poor which plagues Latin America even more than other underdeveloped regions. People with huge holdings own almost all of the land. Growing inequities, along with failure to institute corrective reforms, cause FAO to shy away from estimating the future of food production in Latin America, since "the main constraints . . . appear to be non-technical."

Latin America's higher output, compared to Asia and Africa, should not suggest affluence. Incomes run from a yearly per capita average of about $75 in Haiti to roughly $1,800 in Puerto Rico. The average income in Brazil, a more typical example, is about $450 a year, a figure that appears far worse when the inequality gap is considered. Economic orthodoxies of the recent past, which concentrated development efforts on industry to the neglect of agriculture—partly because this route avoided difficult social reforms—helped to widen that gap.

Like Africa, Latin America has sizable expanses of territory in tropical forests, especially in Brazil; but for Latins, too, the task of making such lands food-producing probably has to be charted in generations, not years. Latin America has much acreage that is underutilized as pasture, or even left idle by wealthy owners who are waiting for values to rise. The solution depends in part upon sweeping changes in land ownership and taxation.

Latin America, too, relies heavily on food exports for earnings. Is it not incongruous that food-deficient nations should export food products to prosperous countries? Coffee, for example, leaches the soil and after several decades leaves it almost useless, while workers labor on the coffee plantations for only a few cents an hour. Yet Latin America uses much of its cultivated acreage for this crop, because it brings vital foreign exchange. Similarly much of Latin America's beef is prepared for export rather than for protein-poor Latins, who cannot afford it.

Peru's fishmeal industry, the largest in the world, provides another example. Although many Peruvians suffer from severe protein deficiencies, this high-protein flour is manufactured not for domestic consumption, but for shipment to Europe and the United States where it feeds livestock. (The United States alone imports more than twice as much fish as the entire underdeveloped world does.) You can understand the desperate need of countries like Peru for export earnings. But the fact that they feel constrained to supply protein to well-fed foreigners, while bypassing their own ill-nourished people, is a disturbing aspect of that large world where hunger is king.

WHAT ABOUT THE FUTURE? The technology of food production can open and expand frontiers, but it cannot work magic. Writers tend to dramatize new methods and give the impression that a cornucopia for everybody is just around the corner. That misleads. Not many more deserts are likely to bloom in the next decades, because usable water is limited—witness the fight of our Southwestern states over rights to existing supplies. Some day the oceans may yield desalted water for transport to the deserts, but the difficulties and cost now are prohibitive. Extending irrigation will continue to be important for increasing food production, but the places suited for this are limited. Environmental backlash is a major restraint on irrigation schemes in many regions.

Private food companies can make an important contribution, but they do not know how to sell food to people who are too poor to buy it. Nutritionist Alan Berg has concluded that

for all the technical ingenuity that has gone into the development of new products, corporate technologists have not yet been able to come up with a food that can be sold commercially for a profit and still be priced low enough to reach and help the masses of people who most need it.

The best known attempt, Incaparina in Guatemala, costs nearly four times more than the cornmeal it replaces.

Nonconventional high-protein foods are certain to become increasingly important, but first much research has to be done, and manufacturing and marketing methods developed. Yeast (fungi) can multiply rapidly on sugary liquids and be turned into a food-stuff or a protein supplement powder. So far it has been used mostly for feeding livestock. Single-cell protein—bacteria that supply half their weight in protein—can be cultivated on products such as petroleum, and may be widely used some day. Single-cell algae have provoked interest, but so far the cost and complications of harvesting them forbid their use as a marketable food. The same applies to microscopic sea life called plankton. British scientists have reportedly found a way of turning starch into a high-protein substance, but experiments have not advanced yet to the point of test-feeding people. Other scientists are searching for ways to extract edible proteins from ordinary grass and leaves.

These pioneering efforts, and others like them, deserve more support than they are getting. At the same time they remind us that the world still depends (and may always depend) overwhelmingly on improvements through conventional methods for feeding its soaring population. Cultivating more land, extending irrigation, development and use of improved varieties, multiple cropping, pest control, fertilizers (only one-fifth of the world's fertilizer output is used in poor countries, and there mainly for export crops), contour plowing, and improved livestock breeding—these are the methods of food production on which the fate of the world's hungry primarily depends.

The most significant attempt so far to project reasonable food production goals has emerged from the United Nations. During the late 1960s the UN Food and Agriculture Organization prepared an *Indicative World Plan* which outlined some achievable targets for the noncommunist underdeveloped countries by 1985. Targets were based not on need but on demand predicted on the basis of population growth and some improved incomes. FAO estimated that from 1962 to 1985 total food production in those countries would have to show an annual increase of 3.9 percent. By 1971 the rate had increased by only 2.8 percent. This barely kept ahead of population growth, yielding only a marginal gain in per capita food production, and meant that production would have to increase each year between 1972 and 1985 by almost 5 percent in order to be on target. Despite this discouraging start, the *Indicative World Plan* shows us what could take place—indeed what has to take place—if even modest gains are to be made.

Its first requirement is a *breakthrough in cereal production,* from 231 million tons in 1962 to 509 million tons (or more than double) by 1985, an annual growth rate of 3.5 percent. Thanks in part to the new high-yield seeds, by 1971 cereal production in underdeveloped countries reached 317 million tons, which put the growth rate for the first nine years almost exactly on target.

FAO's second goal—one that has so far proved elusive—is *to reverse a growing protein gap.* For the short run it emphasizes pig and poultry production, along with high-protein vegetables. For the longer run it anticipates higher yielding varieties of such vegetables, cereals with more protein value, and growth in livestock and fishing. FAO expects the demand for animal and fish protein to run ahead of the supply, which will raise prices and put these proteins still farther out of reach for the poor. Because production of milk will also fall behind demand, the *Indicative World Plan* concludes that "Food aid in processed milk on a massive scale is therefore likely to assume crucial importance, and this appears to be the way in which developed countries could help most in food aid during the 1970s."

Another goal indicated by FAO is *a drastic improvement for underdeveloped countries in agricultural trade,* so they can earn foreign currency essential to their development. To do so, they must become less dependent upon food imports and, FAO estimates, more than double their annual agricultural exports by 1985. This goal, however, exposes a dilemma: although increasing exports makes sense as an overall goal, for many countries it is even more necessary to expand their domestic market for agriculture. For example, would India do better to concentrate on raising nutritional levels and try to earn foreign currency in other ways? I think the answer is yes. But the feasibility of such an approach depends on more enlightened trade and assistance policies on the part of developed countries.

For that matter, even in a nation with more ample food supplies, such as Burma, the FAO goal can be carried out usefully only along with an adequate increase in agricultural production and if the rich nations make changes in their own production and trade policies. For example, the United States is the world's leading exporter of rice, which it subsidizes, a practice that already threatens Burma and Thailand with economic depression. In the long run everybody would benefit if the United States instead emphasized production of high-protein foods, which are increasingly needed in the developing countries. Adjustments required for policy changes of this kind should not and need not be made at the expense of the small U.S. farmer.

So far the trend against improved trade for the underdeveloped countries is ominous. FAO reports that the share of the underdeveloped countries in world agricultural exports dropped from 46 percent in 1955 to 34 percent in 1970, with the rich countries having secured new gains in products such as fats, oils, and rice traditionally exported by the underdeveloped countries. Further, the terms of trade continue to deteriorate. For 1971 the FAO reported a rise of 3 percent in agricultural export prices, but a 6 percent rise in prices for manufactures, giving the poor nations less purchasing power for their agricultural exports.

FAO also hopes for *increased employment in agriculture*—a goal made imperative by the population explosion—and for *general economic development*. The *Indicative World Plan* calls the problem of employment "far more intractable than that of food supply," and perhaps the greatest threat to solving the food problem. In other words, even if the food production goals of the FAO were achieved by 1985—a most unlikely prospect—improved food consumption would take place only among those who are improving themselves economically and could afford to eat better. Unless that happens also among the now-hungry masses, they will be even worse off in 1985, despite statistical gains. *With food production technology putting us theoretically within reach of feeding the world adequately for the first time, the problem is not so much an inability to produce food as it is an inability of the poor to purchase it.* This, in turn, points to the need for major social and economic reforms within underdeveloped countries, as well as for reforms in the way that rich and poor countries deal with each other.

Hunger does not stand alone. It stands within the shadow of poverty. According to Addeke H. Boerma, head of FAO:

It would be futile and unrealistic to attempt to discuss hunger and malnutrition in isolation from other evils of our age such as the stifling clamp of poverty, the flood of overpopulation, the paralysis of unemployment, the deformities of trade. We must look at the economic and social problems of the world in their totality if we are to come to grips with them individually.

To feed hungry people, then, means more than shipping food surpluses abroad. It requires us to sort out hunger's social and economic allies and deal with them in a comprehensive way. To that task this book now turns.

3

The Poor Have More

Almost two centuries ago an Englishman named Thomas Malthus warned that the population would race ahead of the food supply. It would do so, he argued, because we can only *add* to the food supply, while the population *multiplies*. As a schoolboy I joined my classmates in laughing at Malthus, for history had proved him wrong. So I thought. I lived in Oregon, where wide-open spaces seemed only to ridicule the idea of too many people in the world. Besides no one I knew went hungry.

Students in Eugene, Oregon, no longer laugh at Malthus. Wrong in part, he was also partly right.

When I was born in 1928 the world population was on the verge of reaching two billion. It had taken the entire history of the human race from its very beginning until about 1830 to reach the one billion mark. It took a single century to add the second billion. But since then—within the 44 years from my birth—it has added almost two billion more. If I live to the turn of the century I will see a world with still another two or three billion inhabitants. *During one lifetime the earth's living*

45

population will have more than tripled its previous total achievement.

That is an explosion.

It explains why the population graphs show a horizontal line veering suddenly upward—as though a cyclist, riding along a barely noticeable slope, began peddling straight up a cliff.

Graphs and statistics, however, never give us a true picture. Close-up views like this one by Philip Appleman help:

At Sealdah Station, Calcutta, misery radiates outward. In the station, displaced families from East Pakistan hover around little piles of possessions. Outside, dusty streets straggle away in every direction lined with tiny shacks built of metal scraps, pieces of old baskets, strips of wood, and gunny sacks. In the dark interiors of the shacks, small fires glow through the smoke, and dark faces gaze out at children playing in the urinous-smelling, fly-infested streets. In a few years the children who survive these conditions will stop playing and become adults; that is, they will grow taller and thinner and stand in the streets like ragged skeletons, barefoot, hollow-eyes, blinking their apathetic stares out of gray, dusty faces. . . .

. . . Calcutta today, still swollen by millions of refugees until the streets are spotted with their bodies, seems a unique problem; but for the underdeveloped countries at least, it may very well represent the City of the Future.

We have been caught by surprise. During the mid-'30s the U.S. Bureau of Census predicted that the population of the United States would peak at 153 million in 1980, but we are already well on the way to doubling that figure. As late as the 1950s demographers warned of a world population near four billion by the year 2000. We are almost at four billion now. The momentum of growth is great and the braking distance long, like a bus that keeps accelerating in the darkness at unheard-of speeds, and we do not know how well it can stop—or even if it has brakes. If, for example, by the year 2000 parents in the developed countries had only enough children to replace themselves and those who bear no children, and if by the year 2050 the developing nations did the same, the world population would level out at 15 billion people, four times the present density. There is no basis yet for so "optimistic" a forecast.

Will space exploration find a place for a surplus population? No dream could be more futile. The cost alone of transporting perhaps a half million people each day to some unknown planet staggers the mind, to say nothing of the physical complications. We cannot now transport an army one-tenth that size halfway around the world in a day.

Can we pinpoint a maximum feasible population for humanity? We cannot—although the number may be higher if we approach it gradually than if rapid increases provoke massive disruptions. Perhaps in 50 or 100 years hostile areas such as Brazil's Amazon region will hospitably support a huge number of people. If so, that diminishes in no way our need to consider these warning signals:

1. The supply and distribution of food may not keep pace for long with population expansion. If not, we face catastrophic famines and probably other man-made catastrophes.

2. Quadrupling the food, housing, jobs, schools, and public services for four times as many people probably also means quadrupling the hunger, the hovels, the misery.

3. Our human environment is in danger of being irreparably damaged. Lester Brown of the Overseas Development Council believes that we could produce enough food to feed the projected population to the end of the century. "But if we ask 'what are the social and ecological consequences of the rapid advances in farm technology which enable us to sustain past and future increases in population?' we get a very different answer."

4. Politically the world is already in precarious shape and we cannot expect the complications of additional billions to make things easier. We can guess the outcome, at least in part, by seeing what happens now to the mounting number of disinherited urban dwellers. "If a young man cannot find work, his natural reaction is

to blame the socioeconomic system," observes one Latin American. "It is not strange that his energy is spent in resisting the economic and social structures prevalent today."

5. What threat will a population of five, ten, or 20 billion more people pose to individual liberties? The more people there are, the more complex society becomes and pressure builds for more social regulation. The right to privacy, the right to dissent, the right to constitutional protection from both governmental and private interference could—where they exist—easily become casualties. In any case the feeling of the average citizen that he is at the mercy of impersonal forces which he cannot influence will almost certainly increase.

These and other danger signals provide the basis for well-founded concern, especially because we are left to do some guessing in matters that beg for certainty. By now the alarm has been sounded for all to hear: *unless the world soon cuts back the rate of population growth, hunger and poverty will reach unmanageable, catastrophic proportions.*

Considering the extent and implications of the population explosion, this warning assumes the appearance of a self-evident truth. But appearance deceives.

The warning engages in a fantasy of the rich world. The difficulty lies not so much with its accuracy—indeed the warning could be all too accurate. The difficulty lies with the use that it invites. It tends to nourish this fundamental misconception, that the way to check population growth in poor countries is to proclaim the virtues of small families and make birth-control services sufficiently available. But that ignores the key role which hunger and poverty play in spurring growth rates.

The warning also diverts us from coming to grips with hunger and poverty, if it implies—as it often does in context—that we should concentrate mainly on population control, not hunger and poverty. By all evidence this approach is self-defeating, because hunger and poverty virtually guarantee excessive growth rates. Consequently the warning serves us better when it is turned around: *unless we soon cut back on hunger and poverty, population growth will reach unmanageable, catastrophic proportions.*

In the wealthy nations, birth rates diminish during economic recessions, leading many to conclude that poverty discourages population growth. However, a look at our own country shows the highest birth rates occurring among the poor; and the rates are even higher in underdeveloped countries.

It would be a mistake to single out either the reduction of hunger and poverty or the reduction of population growth rates to the exclusion of the other. These goals belong together. Combining them does not necessarily imply a moral judgment in favor of social justice, but it does emphasize an underlying truth about population control: without progress in freeing people from the grip of hunger and poverty, there is little likelihood of restraining a runaway population.

HOW IT
STARTED

This is the way the explosion developed.

About 9000 B.C. the whole earth probably numbered five to ten million people, or roughly the population of New York City. At that time almost everyone hunted or gathered food, so a density of even two persons per square mile could not be supported. The introduction of agriculture gradually revolutionized man's social habits and greatly enlarged the number of people that the earth could feed.

By the time of Christ, the population of the world corresponded roughly to that of the present United States and was growing at the rate of perhaps 2 percent a century. Because disease, war, and famine exacted high claims, life expectancy averaged only 25 to 30 years. Nevertheless, as people cultivated new areas the rate of growth accelerated slowly, despite setbacks such as the bubonic plague which decimated Europe in the fourteenth century.

Midway through the 1600s, shortly after people began migrating to America, the rate of growth started to increase noticeably in Europe. Perhaps a half billion human beings populated the globe then. By the time Malthus published the first edition of his *Essay on Population* in 1798, the total was moving toward a billion and the annual rate of growth had climbed to approximately one-half of 1 percent. The population was fortunate, though. The Industrial Revolution, which began a generation or two before Malthus, arrived early enough to bail people out by providing extra jobs.

Death control—the major cause of today's unprecedented expansion—started after the Industrial Revolution had begun. While Malthus wrote, a fellow Englishman named Edward Jenner was discovering a vaccination for smallpox. This discovery foreshadowed a long series of advances in medicine and public health that over a period of two centuries succeeded dramatically in extending life. Consequently, while new lands and better methods of farming made gains against famine, disease retreated.

The population explosion began in Europe. Not the "inconsiderate masses" of today's poor world, but our European ancestors touched it off. A few simple statistics show this. In 1800 about 22 percent of the human race was Caucasian, but when I was born in 1928 (only five or six generations later) that percentage had jumped to about 35. So until a few decades ago the population boom was primarily a white, Western phenomenon. All that time the European peoples had two enormous advantages:

1. *Industrial growth kept ahead of population increases.* Since gains in public health came slowly during the nineteenth century, epidemics held the population partly in check, and the increase that did occur was usually needed in the cities by industries which depended upon a growing supply of unskilled workers. Although the Industrial Revolution imposed outrageous hardships on people who moved from farms to sweatshops and urban slums, the suffering would have been far greater and the social situation much more explosive had the population raced ahead of industrial jobs.

2. *New lands opened up for colonization.* These new lands, primarily in the Americas, offered an important outlet to the population surpluses that did develop. When the potato famine ruined Ireland, for example, almost a million Irish came to our

shores within five years. When periods of unemployment occurred, the colonies provided an outlet. They also handed Europeans an impressive psychological advantage by keeping hopes alive.

The exact opposite applies to the poor nations today. Public health gains of two centuries, made available to much of the world in a short period of time, cause population figures to begin soaring almost instantly. People pour into the cities long before industry can possibly supply them with jobs; and for all but a few there simply is no frontier, no new lands to colonize, no safety valve. As a result, the population explosion has produced stress and deprivation on a scale without precedent, as well as a momentum of growth that boggles the mind.

Throughout most of history women have had to produce offspring at near capacity in order for the human race to survive and grow just a bit; but now suddenly human fertility threatens to do us in. Not that birth rates are rising. On the contrary they have actually declined slightly for the past several decades in both developed and underdeveloped countries. Thanks to such things as drugs, vaccines, public sanitation, and improved food production, however, the scourges that prevented overpopulation in the past have been reduced. Already underdeveloped nations have more children under the age of 15 than the total population of wealthier nations. By 1980 there will be almost twice as many women in the high-fertility range as there were in 1960. By the turn of the century today's poor nations will make up not two-thirds, but three-fourths of the human family. And projections indicate a world population between six and seven billion by then, with the possibility (in theory, at least) of 15 billion or more by 2035 and 30 billion within a century.

I have already noted that the surge in population occurred first among European peoples, and only later in the countries we now call underdeveloped. Rapid growth began in Europe and spread to North America because public health measures and modern medicine, together with food-producing technologies, gradually lowered the mortality rate. But growth rates were cushioned in the industrialized nations as people became economically more self-sufficient and less dependent upon their offspring for security.

Today the underdeveloped countries have advanced well into the first stage: public health measures and modern medicine have reduced the death rate more rapidly than in the industrialized West, causing their population to multiply faster. *But the second stage is not taking hold.* A majority of people in the poor countries are *not* moving toward the point where their sense of economic improvement and security is clearly related to having fewer children. Instead the opposite usually applies: more children mean more security.

Poor countries can thank us for the population explosion, because rich nations gave them the technology which touched it off. But we have not done much to help them develop economies that can absorb new workers and provide positive incentives for small families. We brought them to stage one and largely deserted them in stage two. As a result the poor countries find themselves locked on the horns of a dilemma.

To a remarkable extent Malthus has triumphed. The population is multiplying beyond his wildest fears, partly because he did not see how science and technology would cut back the death rate and increase food production. But in another sense Malthus had things backward. He considered poverty, disease, and hunger important though regrettable checks on population growth. Therefore he assailed the English "poor laws" on the grounds that they only encouraged the poor to have more children.

History has since contradicted Malthus. Where people are poor, diseased, and hungry, the population soars. Disease and infant mortality have been restrained enough in underdeveloped areas to multiply growth rates—but not enough to assure parents that sons will survive to take care of them in later years. *Once a country begins to reduce its death rate through modern technology, it has to go on to provide social guarantees, or unmanageable growth occurs.* Only when the insecurities of poverty are also reduced do people readily opt for small families. This happened in the

The Poor Have More 53

industrialized countries, and it is beginning to happen in countries like China and Taiwan which are successfully developing. *Where the benefits of healthy economic growth spread sufficiently to the common people, and where the rate of infant mortality approximates that of the rich nations, there people feel secure enough to practice voluntary birth control.* Adequate food, health care, and improved standards of living for the poor emerge as the most fundamental remedy to the population problem.

This does not deny the crucial importance of family birth-control programs. It simply affirms that no country has yet brought a rapidly growing population into balance *primarily* by promoting private methods of control. Conceivably, of course, pressures of growth combined with dramatically improved birth-control methods could change that. But the evidence so far tells us that to expect poor countries to solve their population problem by emphasizing family planning is to nourish an illusion.

ASIA | Asia, where a majority of the human family lives, illustrates the relationship between poverty and the rate of population growth.

Consider India, a classic example of the population boom. During the 30-year period between 1891 and 1921 high birth rates were still largely offset by high death rates, due to famine and disease. Total growth for that entire period was just over 5 percent, or an average of less than one-sixth of 1 percent each year. From 1921 to 1951, however, as famine and epidemics were beaten back, the growth rate multiplied to more than 1 percent a year, and today has climbed to 2.5 percent annually. The birth rate since 1921 actually dropped from 49 to 42 per thousand population; but health protection and food lowered the death rate more dramatically, from 48 to 17 per thousand. Some argue that food and medicine are therefore the real villains to be beaten back. But if starvation and disease do not strike us as acceptable solutions, then we have to look elsewhere.

When India became independent in 1948, its population, not including present-day Pakistan or Bangladesh, stood at 350 million. By 1973 it was approximately 600 million—an increase in one generation alone surpassing the total population of the United States. An unofficial working paper of the Population Division of the United Nations published in 1969 gave this 20-year projection for India:

1965—487 million
1970—555 million
1975—633 million
1980—717 million
1985—807 million

It is easy to see that if anything close to these projections holds true—and so far that appears to be the case—India is racing toward a turn-of-the-century population that will break the one billion mark, and it may not be far behind China by then.

To approximate this phenomenon in terms of numbers alone you would have to crowd all 210 million U.S. citizens into an area one-third the size of the United States. But that is only the beginning. To this land area add Europe's 470 million people, Russia's 250 million, Canada's 22 million, and Mexico's 55 million. Placing all the people of these countries into a small fraction of our own country gives the equivalent, in density, of India with a billion citizens. When we consider the difficulty of preparing for a mere 70 million more U.S. citizens in three decades—with all of our advantages—we can begin to perceive the monumental problem confronting impoverished India. These figures are cold and impersonal, however. We need to translate them into the lives of ordinary people, as one Canadian has done:

A girl in a poor country is a burden to her parents, so she is generally married—one may as well say bought—as soon as she is sexually mature. At an age when she would still be at school in Canada, she is coping with a family. By her twenties, she has several children; she is almost certain to have seen one or more of them die, and maybe has given one to the widow in the next street and left another at the gate of an orphanage; weary of repeated pregnancies, she has probably undermined her health by a couple of back-street abortions, carried out without cleanliness or anaesthetics. In her thirties, she looks like an exhausted old woman.

India's swelling population means women prematurely exhausted and old. It also means Bombay, the most thickly inhabited city in the world, with 115 thousand people to the square mile in 1963—more than four and a half times the density of New York City. Writer Dom Moraes, who was born in Bombay, says that surrounding Bombay's factories are rickety tenements where six or seven workers live in a room. The poorest workers, however, cannot afford even that and camp amidst litter in makeshift huts that consist of four poles and whatever can be attached to them.

This proliferation of shanties and huts is new. It had not existed in my boyhood. But the population of Bombay, when I left it for Europe in 1954, was a million and a half. It is now considerably more than five million, and according to a conservative estimate, more than a million people live in temporary hovels. . . . Occasionally the police force the inhabitants to move on, but like dark snails, their lodgings on their backs, they shift a little way off and set up house once more.

Clerks of the city earning less than a dollar a day cannot afford to live in town, but "have been forced out into the suburbs, where squat, prisonlike blocks of cheap flats have been subsidized by the Government." Those who cannot find accommodations there move still farther out and spend five or six hours a day on train coaches, wedged so tightly into a mass of sweaty bodies that some are forced onto the footboards outside. "On an average," says Moraes, "four of these people fall off every day, and are killed."

With India in such a predicament and with hundreds of millions more on the way, why don't people cut back on reproduction?

Poverty itself works in favor of larger families, because children provide unofficial social security. With a high mortality rate still a factor and starvation never far away, parents know that many children, especially sons, mean protection and care later on. According to India's Minister of State for Family Planning, hunger induces women in his country to produce from eight to ten children on the assumption that only three will survive to become breadwinners. (Good nutrition is therefore "the most realistic contraceptive," he says.) Poor nations that do not provide elementary social security—and they do not because they are poor—inescapably encourage larger families. So the vicious cycle of poverty = more people = more poverty continues to worsen, and it is a difficult circle to break.

In addition poor people no less than others cherish life and have a deep affection for their families. In circumstances that are otherwise hopelessly oppressive, new offspring may give parents an indescribable sense of accomplishment and joy. A father of ten told me proudly, "Children are the one luxury a poor man has."

What about personal birth-control measures? Many parents would have fewer children if information and medical services were available. Because of India's poverty, doctors, nurses, and clinics are in extremely short supply, particularly in rural areas—which is three-fourths of India. An estimated three to four million Indian women undergo illegal abortions each year, a fact which demonstrates some desperation for birth control. Nevertheless, even where India has concentrated control efforts, the results so far have been limited. The experience of the world since the advent of medicine and public health points overwhelmingly to the prospect that as long as poverty prevails, birth-control campaigns will have only a marginal effect on population growth. Thus by far the most effective method of control—short of catastrophic famine, disease, or nuclear war—remains economic and social development for the poor.

Japan, which is even more crowded than India, provides evidence for that conclusion. One hundred seven million people give Japan a total population half that of the United States, but with a land area smaller than California. However, Japan is a rich nation, the industrial giant of Asia, with many advantages. Japan cut its birth rate sharply after World War II, not because of an official birth-control campaign, but because rising levels of income, nutrition, education, and urban development made clear to the average couple that their personal interests would best be served through small families. Inexpensive legal abortions help to curb Japan's population. With a growth rate slightly above the U.S. rate of 1 percent, Japan still adds more than a million people to the rolls every year.

China lies somewhere between India and Japan on the population problem, as well as geographically. China further documents the link between economics and the rate of population growth. With about 750 to 800 million people it comprises one-fifth of mankind. China's population grows by roughly 15 million each year, with rate estimates usually ranging between 1.7 and 2 percent. While that is a formidable annual increase, the rate of growth represents a notable reduction for a country still 85 percent rural, and it compares favorably with India's performance.

What accounts for China's progress? A number of factors contribute, but embracing them all are economic and social guarantees. Although still a poor country, China's resources are so distributed that every citizen is entitled to the essentials of life, including food, housing, and health care. Large families, however, mean more hardship rather than extra security.

In addition China has campaigned for birth control since 1954, except for a lapse that began in 1958 when Chairman Mao announced (along orthodox Marxist lines and as part of the Great Leap Forward) that all additional manpower could be put to good use for the country. China, however, experienced food shortages and a severe economic setback from 1959 to 1961, so the birth-control campaign resumed. China experts have attributed that country's success in slowing the growth rate to postponement of marriage, the assignment of medical personnel to rural areas, the training of "barefoot doctors" for birth-control services, and the fact that young adults coming up now have been indoctrinated from childhood by the revolutionary government. (These are practices which an authoritarian form of government like China's obviously finds easier to establish than does a democracy like India.) The underlying control, in any case, seems to be a dependable, if stringent, system of social and economic security.

Other countries of Asia fit the pattern of showing poverty's contribution to population growth. In South Korea and Taiwan birth rates dropped sharply as living standards for the poor began to improve substantially, and this happened *in advance of* active birth-control programs. For example, Taiwan's birth rate fell from 46 per thousand in 1952 to 31 per thousand in 1963. That year an official birth-control program was vigorously adopted, but the birth rate has fallen only slightly since then, a decrease that may be due more to economic and social gains than to family-planning programs.

Many poor countries have higher per capita incomes, but poorer distribution of incomes and social services than South Korea and Taiwan. Consequently they also have much higher population growth rates. In 1971 Brazil's per capita income was $395, South Korea's $280. But in Brazil the income ratio of the richest 20 percent to the poorest 20 percent was 25 to 1, while in South Korea the ratio was only 5 to 1. Brazil also had higher rates of illiteracy, infant mortality, and unemployment. Both countries had population growth rates of 3 percent in 1958, but by 1971 Brazil's held at 2.9 percent, while South Korea's had dropped to 2 percent. South Korea had the advantage of a birth-control program, but like Taiwan, most of its drop coincided with social and economic improvements for the poor and came *prior* to the control programs.

Elsewhere in Asia heavily populated countries include Indonesia, with 130 million people, Pakistan, with 68 million, and Bangladesh, with 81 million. As a group, these three countries are about as poor as India and average a population increase in excess of 3 percent a year.

AFRICA | Africa, a sizable continent with one-fifth of the
world's land mass and relatively few people, might
appear to have escaped the problem of overpopulation. Regrettably,
that is not the case. Both desert and tropics present formidable obstacles to the support of human life, so the question is one of food,
not square miles. Africa faces the same difficulty that besets other
underdeveloped areas: poverty denies parents the security and incentive they need in order to practice voluntary birth control. Consequently, limited economic gains get swallowed by additional
people.

Egypt, growing at the rate of nearly 3 percent a year, expects to
more than double its 37 million people by the turn of the century,
the food-producing benefits of the Aswan Dam project wiped out
many times by then. Nigeria's 59 million will have swollen past
the 120 million mark. While these two nations, in terms of sheer
numbers, express overpopulation most acutely, smaller African
countries by no means escape the dilemma. Kenya, for example,
consistently advances each year by 6 or 7 percent in economic
output; but with half of its population below the age of fifteen,
unemployment spreads, as young people leave the farms and
plantations for the cities.

Despite these signals African policy-makers frequently brush
aside the population problem to stress exploitation of that continent's rich resources and the need for more manpower which new
technology will require. Such an optimistic stance may be justified
in certain regions. In addition, as Africa develops its resources and
modernizes, a larger population will be desirable. But it is one
thing for the population to keep pace with modernizing opportunities, and quite another for it to race ahead. The report of the
Pearson Commission on International Development* said that the
most widespread misconception about population among leaders in
low-income countries is the belief that in small or sparsely settled
nations rapid increase is in the national interest. "This proposi-

* Hereafter referred to as the Pearson report or the Pearson commission.

tion," the report goes on to say, "neglects the fact that large capital expenditures are necessary for cultivation and settlement in empty land—in the modern world, the possession of land is not enough."

Leaders caught up in the spirit of youthful nationalism find it understandably difficult to think in terms of restraining population growth. Yet the lessons of the recent past tell us that the closer today's 370 million Africans approach to becoming 800 million by the turn of the century, the more difficult it will be for them to avoid becoming hopelessly mired in hunger, joblessness, and urban chaos. Yet the fact that most Africans *are* impoverished prevents them from applying the brakes on rapid population growth.

LATIN AMERICA | Dr. Alfredo Aguirre, a pediatrician in Colombia who has specialized in family planning, describes the poor Colombian family as one that is "plagued by hunger, misery, and ignorance, with each of these elements made worse by an increasing number of children for whom there is neither the means nor even the desire to satisfy basic needs." Circumstances, he says, may force mothers, consciously or unconsciously, to practice "masked infanticide" in which

. . . children between six months and four years of age are often allowed to die when attacked by any disease, particularly diarrhea. We have even seen mothers who objected to their children being treated and, in the same vein, were upset when curative measures were successful. No less rarely, such children are abandoned in the hospital, presenting a difficult problem. A frequent indication of "masked infanticide" is apparent when a mother or a couple of very limited means approaches the physician for a "death certificate" for their child without any emotion or sense of anguish. . . .

Colombia illustrates the people boom in Latin America. With a population of four million in 1900, Colombia now has 23 million, and by the time the century is ended it is expected to have about 56 million. Colombia reflects Latin America, whose projected population of 650 million by the year 2000 would give it an increase of more than 1,000 percent this century—to say nothing of what the next century might bring. Not that Latin America is incapable of supporting 650 million persons. Given enough time for overall development, it could accommodate more than that. Latin America is not capable, however, of handling a human tidal wave, and there is no prospect of holding it back, as long as the lack of bare necessities robs people of security.

Two predictable consequences of this tidal wave are revolution and repression. Another may have been foreshadowed in the "Soccer War" of 1969 between Honduras and El Salvador (a war preceded by rioting over soccer games between these Central American neighbors). "Space war" would be a more accurate designation. El Salvador's 3.5 million people are jammed into 8,260 square miles, compared with Honduras's 2.5 million in 43,277 square miles. For several decades approximately 300,000 Salvadorans crossed the border seeking land and jobs. The squeeze turned friendship into hostility and violence.

Another consequence of the human tidal wave in underdeveloped nations is the widespread practice of illegal abortion. That practice prompted Chile some years ago to become one of the few Latin American governments to promote family-planning measures. Dr. Herman Romero, professor of preventive medicine at the University of Chile, estimates that abortion may be induced in up to half of the pregnancies in that country. Dr. Benjamin Viel, a colleague of Romero's, points out that these abortions increase with urbanization. They are most common with middle-class women who can afford to pay a low fee—with risks usually in proportion to the price. Among the poor, says Dr. Viel, "a woman is likely to perform a crude abortion on herself by inserting a stiff implement or sewing needle through the neck of the uterus. She seeks help only when hemorrhaging begins." This practice causes many deaths. Why not legalize abortions? Aside from moral objections, Dr. Viel writes, it would be impractical, because Chile does not have enough doctors or hospital beds to handle the demand.

What should Latin America do about its rapid population

growth? Your answer probably depends on whether you live here or there. In September, 1966, the Committee for Economic Development issued two reports that dealt with the problem. The report prepared by a committee of 44 North Americans urged birth-control programs. The other, prepared by nine Latin Americans and one U.S. citizen, favored improved nutrition and reduced infant mortality—with the U.S. member registering a dissent. Commenting on these reports, ecologist Barry Commoner notes:

. . . the Latin Americans wish to pursue, for themselves, the course toward population balance that the advanced nations have followed—increased living standards, reduced mortality, followed by the commonly experienced reduction in birth rate. For their part, the North Americans are urging on the poorer nations a path toward demographic balance that no society in human history, certainly not their own, has ever followed. . . .

THE UNITED STATES | We need to disabuse ourselves of the idea that the population boom is primarily a problem of the poor nations. It is our problem, too. That is true above all in the sense that the industrialized nations exported it to the poor countries. This they did primarily by introducing public health and medical practices which set back the death rate, but without building an economic base that would make voluntary family planning work. On the contrary, the North Atlantic countries have a long history of extracting wealth from the poor nations. Now we are in a position to help them break the poverty-population cycle by massive support for global development. Failing this, we have no one to blame but ourselves. Asians, Africans, and Latins will increasingly charge us with wanting *them* to practice birth control, so that the United States can continue to hold a lion's share of world wealth and power.

But the population problem is ours also because of our own growth.

When I was born in 1928, Eugene, Oregon, had a population

of 17,000. Today Eugene has 80,000, and the metropolitan area twice that many people. When the century began Eugene had 3,000 people; but if it continues to grow at the present rate, by the time the century ends it will house about 200,000. Eugene could easily become the center of an urban mass numbering a million people while my not-as-yet-arrived grandchildren are still alive. From my father's birth to my grandchildren's demise is an extraordinarily short period of time to leap from 3,000 to one million people. No wonder that Governor Tom McCall of Oregon tells out-of-staters, "Come and visit us, but whatever you do, don't move here."

Madison County, Illinois, where I now live, had a population of about 165,000 when I moved there in 1946. Today it numbers 260,000, and by the year 2000 it should be moving toward the half-million mark. Madison County includes part of the industrial area east of St. Louis, so like Eugene its growth reflects migration to urban centers more than it does the national increase.

This growing concentration of people in urban areas exposes the primary population problem within the United States: failure to distribute our population on a rational basis. For the past several decades more than half the counties in the United States *dropped* in total population, while urban centers acted like magnets. For example, Illinois's population grew by 10 percent between 1960 and 1970, yet 49 of the state's 102 counties lost population. According to the Urban Land Institute, by the year 2000, 55 percent of the nation's people will be living in three strip cities: one along the eastern seaboard from above Boston to south of Washington, D.C.; another along the base of the Great Lakes from Green Bay, Wisconsin, to Utica, New York; and a third in California from San Francisco to the Mexican border. Size can mean economy—up to a point; but beyond that point diseconomies show up in such things as time and expense of commuting, urban-freeway construction, distribution of electricity, and waste disposal. And the social costs may exceed the economic costs.

The strange thing is that this urban concentration has occurred with virtually no debate, as the outcome of uncontrolled technology, and not because most people wanted it that way. Mechanization drove people off the farms and out of rural areas to the cities where jobs were available. Far from being a matter of choice, the migration has been forced. In a sense executives of industry who built where they could find raw materials, markets, lower transportation costs, and other advantages had no free choice either. But industry did not pay for and no one counted the social and economic costs of urban slums. To a large extent, the government helped to finance this unplanned population shift through such methods as FHA loans, highway subsidies, restricted agricultural production, and urban renewal.

The government had a population distribution program in the past, when it decided to settle the West, and it can have one again. Better distribution is within reach partly because many industries are no longer so dependent upon particular locations, but also because we have seen the consequences of not dealing with poverty and joblessness where they have occurred. The National Goals Research Staff tells us what will happen if we let the present trends go on:

> Hundreds of American towns will continue to lose young people and economic opportunity; and the large metropolitan areas, already burdened with social and fiscal problems and characterized by fragmentation of governmental responsibility, may reach a size at which they will be socially intolerable, politically unmanageable and economically inefficient.

We don't have to let the trends tell us what to do. We can selectively enlarge many of our old communities and we can build new towns. This will happen, however, not merely by our wishing that it would, but only if the President and Congress hammer out programs that bring it about.

Even with well-planned distribution, however, we would still face sizable population increases. In a special message to Congress on the population problem—the first of its kind in our history—President Nixon echoed a forecast of 300 million U.S. inhabitants by the turn of the century. It took us 300 years to 1917 for the first 100 million, only 50 years to 1967 for the second 100 million, and the third would come, he said, in about 30 years. But in 1972 the U.S. Bureau of Census reported that for a nine-month period the country's fertility rate had, for the first time, fallen below the replacement level. Although this may have been partly a reflex prompted by the recession, it led to speculation that our turn-of-the-century population might fall 30 million short of the predicted 300 million, although that would still mean a large increase. The difference of one extra child per family is startling. For example, if families average two children, and immigration remains stable, the U.S. population total will exceed 340 million a hundred years from now. If, however, families average three children, the population will reach nearly *one billion* by then.

More than numbers are at stake. Additions to our country exact a far greater toll from nature than an equal number of additions to an underdeveloped country. Nutritionist Jean Mayer writes:

> Rich people occupy much more space, consume more of each natural resource, disturb the ecology more, and create more land, air, water, chemical, thermal and radioactive pollution than poor people. So it can be argued that from many viewpoints it is even more urgent to control the numbers of the rich than it is to control the numbers of the poor.

This argument deserves cautious handling, because the largest share of responsibility for environmental deterioration should be laid not to population increases or to increased use of resources, but rather to highly polluting methods of production. That being the case it seems unfair to expect the not yet born to make up for our bad industrial habits by staying out of existence. On the other hand, even if our most polluting technologies are revised, U.S. citizens will make much higher demands on the physical environment than their counterparts in India for at least many decades.

What about the effect of growing numbers on the quality of life? I am not sympathetic with those who cite overpopulation as the principle cause of "ungovernable" cities, jammed freeways, drug abuse, crime, strain on family life, growth of impersonal bureaucracies, ineffective schools, mental illness, and the like. These problems have solutions that need to be hammered out in the public arena, and we prevent ourselves from doing so by letting "population" become the scapegoat. It is fair to add, however, that population increases make these problems more difficult. There are other intangibles, such as young people feeling lost in the shuffle. When I was nineteen I borrowed $3,500, bought some old printing equipment, and started a newspaper; but opportunities like this are diminishing. Today the average congressman represents 483,000 people; a generation from now he will represent 150,000 more. This growing distance between the ordinary citizen and those who govern him also illustrates the toll of numbers on our life.

How can we deal with the U.S. population growth rate?

1. *End poverty.* Poor people average more children per family than those above the poverty line. One of the best population-control programs for the United States would be to raise the living standard of those with low incomes.

2. *Promote the ideal of two children per family.* Adults whose needs and abilities are not satisfied with just two might consider alternative ways of sharing life, such as adoption of "hard to place" children, or foster care. The government could encourage this ideal through modest tax incentives.

3. *Step up research.* We are decades behind schedule and there is not a moment to lose. Medical science, which did so much to cause the population boom, should develop a variety of new methods that provide simple, inexpensive, and dependable control. These would benefit the whole world. Dr. John Morris of Yale University reports, "I've never been in a field in which the harvest is ready to be reaped so easily. So much is yet unknown that almost any experiment you can devise finds an answer that nobody has gotten before." In 1971 about $65 million was spent worldwide on reproductive biology research, although three times that much is needed each year for a decade. In fiscal year 1972 the administra-

tion used only half of the money Congress had authorized for this purpose.

4. *Educate.* The first national workshop on population education was held in 1970, and it attracted only 50 teachers. An analysis of various primary and secondary textbooks reveals an almost complete blank on the subject. According to the Population Reference Bureau, "To the extent that population problems are discussed in the schools, they are overwhelmingly set down as the burden of the developing nations." Such a bias ignores our own extensive contribution, and that of other rich nations, to the population boom in those countries. It also fails to deal with population problems within the United States.

5. *Provide better access to medical services.* Since those most handicapped for lack of information and service are in the low-income bracket, they would benefit the most from wider access.

By far the most important thing we can do toward slowing down *world* population growth is to cooperate extensively with poor countries in helping them improve economic and social conditions. As long as hunger stalks these lands and people depend on offspring for security, populations are virtually certain to spiral upward. Those who expect effective control without economic development fantasize.

I have assumed the possibility of voluntary restraints. Increasingly we hear warnings that voluntarism will no longer do, that family planning means having as many children as you want, which will give the world an overpopulation of many billions. I stick to a voluntary approach for these reasons: (1) A fundamental human right and human dignity are at stake. (2) We cannot speak of the failure of voluntarism until it has been tried— tried with a fully educated public, accessible family services, improved methods of control, and above all changed living conditions for the world's poor. (3) When coercion is pushed, expect a backlash. The poor of the world will see signs of genocide, especially if we remain unwilling to deal with the poverty that provokes them to higher birth rates. In short, coercion is not right and can have an effect quite the opposite from the intended one. As Frank Notestein, former President of the Population Council, has observed, coercive measures are "more likely to bring down the government than the birth rate."

I have skirted the question of abortion not because it is irrelevant, but because it is too complex for fair treatment here. Arguments on both sides tend to oversimplify, and you are left with the impression that induced abortion is either premeditated murder or as morally neutral as removing a wart. In each case the argument depends on an unproved assumption about when a human life begins (at conception? at or near birth?). Frankly I am concerned about the ease with which the question of human life and the right of life is so quickly brushed aside by many who otherwise are in the forefront of concern for human rights—although clearly a balance of rights is involved here. On the other hand I am disturbed that voices most eloquent on behalf of the unborn frequently remain silent about the millions upon millions of people, young and old, who without intervening help are doomed to a life of hunger, neglect, and misery. In the United States the issue has been partially resolved by the U.S. Supreme Court; but morally abortion will remain for many an unacceptable action or an agonizing dilemma. The greatest cause of abortion is poverty itself, together with the nonavailability to the poor of birth-control methods that are simple, acceptable, and effective.

Opposition of the Roman Catholic Church to the use of contraceptives is a factor of major importance in terms of world population. While the church's official position is clear, it is no secret that at every level there are great internal differences over this issue. Studies show that almost as many Roman Catholics use "the pill" as do their Protestant and Jewish counterparts in the United States. In his encyclical of 1968, *Humanae Vitae,* Pope Paul VI reiterated the church's traditional stand against contraceptives—two years after a special Papal Commission on the matter recommended a change. During that two-year period the Pope had issued another encyclical, *Development of the Peoples,* which deals with the matter in a way which probably comes closer to informing the attitude of most U.S. Catholics today. He wrote:

Finally, it is for the parents to decide, with full knowledge of the matter, on the number of their children, taking into account their responsibilities toward God, themselves, the children they have already brought into the world, and the community to which they belong. In all this they must follow the demands of their own conscience enlightened by God's law authentically interpreted, and sustained by confidence in Him.

Regardless of the eventual outcome of this issue in Catholic teaching and practice, finding ways now of making the rhythm method of birth control reliable would enable many more Roman Catholics throughout the world to plan smaller families. Cardinal Terence Cooke of New York has said, "Major efforts [in population control] should be directed to research and the development of a sufficiently certain and morally acceptable solution to the problem."

Looking over the wide range of factors at work in the population explosion today, you find it hard to be optimistic, but attitudes are changing. As recently as 1960 only three underdeveloped nations had population-control policies, and no international development agency did work in family planning. By 1973 most of Asia and a handful of countries elsewhere had official population programs, although modest in scope, and several international agencies gave financial assistance to the developing countries for this purpose. Still, birth-control research and services are badly underfunded, even in the United States, and our own government's leadership in population planning falls short on most counts.

One fact stands above all others.

The United States fails on the global level by not supporting a program of economic development that would enable the poor of the world to achieve security, without which birth-control efforts are doomed to fail. As a result, we reinforce the dilemma: populations racing ahead of economic development lack the most elementary guarantees for decent living; and so far no country has slowed itself out of the population race without the incentive of distributed economic and social gains.

Meanwhile, poverty continues to push the population swiftly upward, and with it the number of hungry people.

4

A Widening Gap

People go hungry because they are poor. We cannot come to terms with hunger unless we deal with poverty. And we cannot understand poverty apart from a rapidly growing gap between the haves and the have nots of the world.

Poverty in most countries defies the imagination. Peter Drucker has said:

> What impresses the outside world about the United States today is not how our rich men live—the world has seen riches before, and on a larger and more ostentatious scale. What impresses the outside world is how the poor of this country live. "Up to Poverty" is the proper slogan for the great world-wide vision and improvement.

Drucker has a point. Where in our own cities do you see—as you can in India—people carrying buckets of water from or bathing at public water taps, emaciated cattle wandering in the streets, women scooping up piles of dung for use as fuel, children picking out undigested grains from the dung for food, people sleeping in the streets, urinating in the streets, begging in the streets, competing for garbage in the streets, and dying in the streets?

71

British journalist Dennis Bloodworth tells of the time he first brought his oriental wife Ping to London. "Don't show me more museums," she told him, "Show me poor people. I want to see how poor people in West live." So Bloodworth showed her the slums of London, only to find her exasperated. "No," she protested, "You don't understand, I mean poor people, *reary* poor people."

Not only is the poverty of most nations far worse than that within the United States, but today those nations cannot hope to climb to prosperity by repeating our experience. Scientist Georg A. Borgstrom makes this evaluation:

Few undertakings in human history have had a greater impact than the enormous, prolonged effort to Europeanize the world. The psychological investment in this drive may explain both the West's lofty promises of abundance for all men and its complete misjudgment of mankind's true situation. In truth, the white man's experience has been misleading. No group of individuals ever seized a greater booty than did the Europeans who took possession of the vast forests and rich prairie soils of the North American continent. Unassuaged, the white man also grabbed the fertile pampas and most other good soils in Central and South America, the South African veld and the rich highland plateaus of the interior Africa. He managed to gain control of an entire continent, Australia, with its valuable satellite, New Zealand. In addition, he secured strongholds all over Asia where he monopolized trade and to a considerable degree controlled agricultural production. . . .

Western empire building, which devoured most of the world, had a far different meaning for the conquered people than it had for the conquerors. For example Bengal (today's Bangladesh and the West Bengal state of India), the first territory of British conquest in Asia, was a prosperous province with highly developed centers of manufacturing and trade, and an economy as advanced as any prior to the Industrial Revolution. Plunder and heavy land taxes reduced Bengal to poverty, as did uneven trade arrangements that barred competitive Indian goods from England, but gave

British goods free entry into India. India's late Prime Minister Nehru commented bitterly, "Bengal can take pride in the fact that she helped greatly in giving birth to the Industrial Revolution in England." British rule became comparatively enlightened and brought some advances to India such as Western science. But the North Atlantic powers seized territories and privileges to enrich themselves, not to benefit the local population.

New lands not only boosted Western economic development, but they also provided a safety valve for Europe's growing population. We can imagine the burden for Europe if all its living descendants—virtually the entire population of the United States, Canada, much of Latin America, plus Australia and some European colonies in Asia and Africa—were compressed into Europe. North America in particular was a huge breadbasket waiting to be farmed, a storehouse of natural resources made to order for the Industrial Revolution.

Lester B. Pearson, the late Prime Minister of Canada, reminded us what a difference these advantages made when the North Atlantic nations were struggling to develop:

One hundred fifty years ago, most economies doubted the capacity of the new Atlantic-European industrial system of that epoch to survive. What transformed mid-century gloom into the long Victorian boom was, above all, the opening up for settlement by Atlantic peoples of the world's remaining, virtually unoccupied belt of fertile temperate land. This biggest bonanza ever bestowed upon a single group was purchased for little more than the cost of running the Indians and the Aborigines and the Bantu off their ancestral lands. It temporarily ended the Malthusian nightmare of population growth outstripping resource availability. Its vast input of almost "free" resources took the Atlantic countries past the borders of modernization and into the new territory of "sustained growth." Nothing comparable is available to developing nations today—unless we use our abundant capital and technology to provide a comparable form of aid relevant to our times. If we say they must develop without it, then we are really abandoning them to permanent helplessness and poverty.

Pearson added, "Their nineteenth-century bonanza gave the Atlantic peoples, representing less than 20 percent of the world's population, a grip on the planet's resources which they have since maintained and even strengthened."

Today's poor nations have no comparable outlet for their populations, which are increasing far more rapidly than Europe's ever did. They do not have the input of wealth, science, and energy that characterized growth in Europe and North America, an input obtained in part at the expense of the poor nations. They face the difficult task of pulling themselves up from poverty at a point in history when forces are sucking them deeper into it.

In these countries most migration occurs not to lands of opportunity, but to cities of last resort. Until recently cities in Europe and North America have grown along with industries that supplied jobs. But poor countries now experience the opposite: peasants pour into cities far in advance of employment opportunities. Too few industries exist, and some hire only skilled workers because they are already automated. "Hands" are no longer as marketable as they were earlier in our own history.

U.S. citizens clearly build on unparalleled advantages. The merchants, farmers, factory workers, and housewives of my home town enjoy a level of prosperity that is possible only because the past has granted us unprecedented favors. Inherited economic and social advantages, not an imagined moral superiority, explain why the average personal income in the United States reached $4,581 in October, 1972, a figure that would amount to $18,324 a year for a family of four—and these figures are expected to double well before the turn of the century. Because earnings are unevenly distributed, a majority of U.S. families earn far under $18,324. But even taking this into account, the fact remains that hungry people of the world do not have access to the advantages that paved the way for these achievements.

In comparing rich and poor nations today we are pressed to use the crude measuring device of either per capita national output

(Gross National Product) or per capita income. But the U.S. GNP includes research and development of highly polluting technologies, as well as the cost of repairing the environmental damage caused by those technologies. Both are counted as part of the nation's output, although one should be subtracted from the other. Similarly, traffic jams raise the GNP by boosting gasoline sales, auto repairs, and medical expenses. GNP figures also distort in the sense that a haircut in the United States costs roughly 15 times the price of a haircut in India—but a haircut is a haircut. Despite these distortions, per capita figures provide us with a fairly clear idea of where wealth and poverty are concentrated.

The Pearson report estimates that 34 percent of the world's population has more than 87 percent of its Gross National Product. That leaves two-thirds of the human race with less than 13 percent of the world's output. Further, under this breakdown "rich" nations include countries that by our standards are poor. An industrial worker in Russia, for example, worked 10 times as long as his American counterpart in 1971 to purchase a refrigerator, 17 times as long to purchase an orange, 9 times as long for a dozen eggs, and 4 times as long for a pound of beef. Compared to the extreme poverty of underdeveloped countries, however, the U.S.S.R. is properly classified as wealthy.

In 1971 GM sales of $28 billion exceeded the GNP of all but four underdeveloped countries (Brazil, China, India, and Mexico). AT&T's gross operating revenues of $18.5 billion surpassed the output of every country in Africa, and of Pakistan and Bangladesh combined. Ford ranked well ahead of Egypt, Indonesia, Nigeria, and the Philippines. When countries and multinational companies are ranked together on the basis of total production, about 40 of the top 100 are companies, most of them headquartered in the United States, and all of them higher producers than a majority of underdeveloped countries. The *increase alone* of $102 billion in U.S. output for 1972 outstripped the *total* output of every poor country, with the possible exception of China. Our increase that year exceeded the entire productive capacity of India, Indonesia, Bangladesh and Pakistan combined (population 875 million), as well as that of all Africa.

Moving away from GNP's, other comparisons reveal the same lopsidedness. Prudential and Metropolitan insurance companies together have as much life insurance in force as the entire poor world (without China) has income. Pakistan, with almost 70 million people, has a national budget of $608 million, while the State of Illinois, without the foreign and defense obligations that corner most of Pakistan's budget, has budgeted $7 billion for 11 million people. Illinois will spend more than twice as much for highway construction and maintenance than Pakistan will for its entire budget.

Even more distressing than the *size* of the gap between rich and poor nations is that the gap continues to increase, not only in total amounts, but in *percentages* as well. Two centuries ago the average per capita income of the richest countries was perhaps eight times greater than that of the poorest. But today's average U.S. citizen has an income level probably a hundred times that of his counterparts in Bangladesh. India's per capita income went from about $64 in 1953 to $88 in 1970, while in the United States the figures for those years jumped from $2,100 to $4,274. In underdeveloped countries as a whole from 1960 to 1970 the average per capita income increased by 27 percent, compared to 43 percent in developed countries.

The distinction between increases in *total* amounts of growth and *percentages* of growth is critical, because only with regard to the latter can poor countries even hope to make gains on rich ones. Narrowing the gap in terms of total amounts is not mathematically possible for many years without virtually stopping growth in the rich countries, a condition that would almost certainly have damaging repercussions in the poor nations. For example, per capita income in the United States is about 50 times that of India, so a 1 percent per capita growth here means an annual increase of roughly $45 per person on the average, while a growth rate ten times higher in India would only increase incomes by about $9 per person.

Suppose that the picture were suddenly reversed, and from now on underdeveloped countries as a group sustained a per capita growth rate twice that of the rich countries. *The income gap would still continue to widen for about 86 years.* If the same growth rates persisted beyond that point, however, the gap would close completely after an additional 35 years. Clearly for the next several decades a narrowing of the gap in real terms seems out of the question, and to suggest otherwise nourishes illusory hopes. But we could tip the *percentages* of per capita growth in favor of the poor countries.

As alarming as the income disparities *between* rich and poor nations is the fact that gap-widening usually takes place *within* poor countries as well, where the affluent few absorb most of the gain. Rapid population growth accelerates this trend by depressing wages through an oversupply of workers and by inflating land values and rents, as space becomes harder to secure. A widening income gap within underdeveloped countries shrinks already limited annual gains to pennies for the poor, and in many cases makes their situation even worse than before. Partly because of this "severely skewed income distribution" the World Bank concluded in its 1972 annual report: "As a generality, it is probably true that the world's burden of poverty is increasing rather than declining."

The growing maldistribution of income both between nations and within nations sharpens Lester B. Pearson's warning that our planet cannot survive "half-slave, half-free, half-engulfed in misery, half-careening along toward the supposed joys of almost unlimited consumption."

Part II

THE WAY OUT

5

The Development Struggle

In *The Hungry Future* Bernard Rosier writes, "One thing cannot be emphasized too strongly: the war against hunger and malnutrition can be waged successfully only if it is treated as one component part of an active policy for overall economic development." Because hunger springs from poverty, gains against hunger require development, the kind of development that enables the poor to achieve economic and social improvements.

THE RECORD SO FAR Despite a rapidly widening income gap, the outlook for underdeveloped countries is not yet one of despair. The record of the past two and a half decades indicates the uncertain position these countries are in. On the one hand development achievements fail to indicate a favorable outcome for them; but on the other hand those achievements do show the *possibility* of such an outcome. The Pearson commission, for example, singled out the limited goal of self-sustaining economic growth and asked whether a majority of underdeveloped countries

lester b. pearson
journal of internat'l
affairs, no.2, 1970
p. 159

could achieve that goal by the end of the century. It replied:

> . . . The answer is clearly yes. In our view, the record of the past twenty years justifies that answer. We live at a time when the ability to transform the world is only limited by faintness of heart or narrowness of vision. We can now set ourselves goals that would have seemed chimerical a few decades ago and, working together, we can reach them.

Unfortunately the above statement, by itself, appears to exaggerate the role of economic growth and to play down more important goals aimed at human welfare. Nevertheless, the record of economic growth has been impressive, because, excluding communist nations, the underdeveloped countries as a group averaged an increase of 5 percent a year during the 1960s—the first UN Development Decade. The importance of this is underscored by the fact that the overall growth rate of the underdeveloped countries surpassed that which the rich countries achieved when they were in the earlier stages of development. In short, we have witnessed an unprecedented accomplishment, one that would not have been possible without a new episode in history: the rise of international cooperation in development since World War II.

That episode began when the United States sent billions of dollars worth of assistance annually to Europe under the Marshall Plan starting in 1948. The Marshall Plan proved at once so helpful that in 1949 President Truman proposed to the U.S. Congress a program of assistance for underdeveloped countries. At the same time Truman appealed to the United Nations, which quickly set up an Expanded Program of Technical Assistance, now part of the UN Development Program. As the European countries and Japan became economically strong, they changed from recipient nations to donor nations, thus gradually increasing the flow of funds to underdeveloped areas.

How many people have been able to buy food and clothes, go to school, work and get medical care as a result of this? Hundreds of millions, and they are the real measure of this global effort.

Among other accomplishments is the expansion of economic

development as a practical science. Over the years a number of strategies have emerged: one emphasized big industry; another, industries that substitute national products for those being imported. Others concentrated on technical assistance, or on key sectors such as agriculture or education. Some stressed social reforms, others balanced growth. In carrying out these sometimes contradictory approaches under a wide variety of conditions, understanding and competence in development have greatly increased. I am barely suggesting the intellectual energy that for more than two decades has concentrated on development throughout the world, though collectively it does not match the intellectual concentration devoted to our voyages to the moon.

During the past 25 years tens of thousands of experts in various aspects of development have been trained; nations and international agencies have worked together on a scale previously unknown; and a rich backlog of knowledge has been assembled. So while most of the poor countries were shaking off some form of colonial domination and finding their independence, they also began digging into the extremely complex problems of development, and have on the whole advanced remarkably both in technical know-how and in self-reliance. This has shown up in many of their annual growth rates. Because the United States played a central role in opening a large flow of assistance to underdeveloped countries, we naturally find gratification in the gains those countries have made.

Unfortunately the development story also contains a deeply ironic twist. The optimism and determination that characterized the early 1960s, symbolized by John F. Kennedy's vision of ending hunger by the end of the decade, turned to caution and malaise. Many things contributed to this change, not least the debilitating cost of the war in Vietnam. Despite extraordinary accomplishments, by 1973 underdeveloped countries were in many ways worse off than before. Accomplishments have sometimes fostered problems more intractable than that of economic growth.

Unemployment, which may contribute more to hunger than

inadequate food production, provides an outstanding example. Unemployment is climbing swiftly in most underdeveloped countries, even where economies are growing at a high rate. This defies a long-held assumption that sufficient job opportunities naturally follow a rapidly growing economy. Why this change? One reason is that the cost of creating new jobs has greatly increased. Another is the size of the labor force, swollen by population growth and rapidly rising. When the decade began, for example, India added a net gain of roughly 100,000 each week to its labor force; by the end of the 1970s, the weekly increase will average about 140,000. When Europe and the United States were industrializing, economic growth rates of 2 to 3 percent provided enough nonagricultural jobs to fully absorb increases in the labor force. But according to a World Bank estimate, the growth rate necessary for the same achievement in underdeveloped countries today would average slightly above 10 percent. As Brazil shows, even that is no guarantee.

Because other development problems seem almost as stubborn, the first Decade of Development left most poor nations deeply disappointed. Population expansion had wiped out half the value of their 5 percent annual growth rate, and other factors combined to offset much of the rest.

OBSTACLES TO DEVELOPMENT

We need to examine some of the factors that prevent or distort healthy economic development, including those that appear to be strictly internal matters. Unless we understand the struggle poor nations face, our policies will reflect ignorance, and ignorance leads us to compound their problems.

The first internal obstacle to development is attachment to the status quo. As experience in development grows, so does understanding within poor countries about reforms of national policies and customs that are necessary. But leaders may find it too difficult, politically hazardous, or against their personal interest to press for action—reasons which prevent leaders in the United States as well from carrying out badly needed reforms. Speeches or toothless laws may be offered instead of reforms, and foreign assistance can even provide an opportunity for postponing changes urgently needed. A rigid class system, an ethic which demeans common labor, and the concentration of land in the hands of wealthy owners are examples of traditions that can cause a country to stagnate. So are inefficient bureaucracies, corruption among government officials, and tax laws that heavily favor the rich. A program to change these things, however, is a program for social upheaval.

Among poor people, their stagnating attitudes and practices reflect failure to understand the causes of poverty. When an awakening takes place regarding these causes, it constitutes a powerful force for development. It is also a potentially explosive force, because people who no longer passively accept their lot in life, but consider it unjust, will determine to change it, sometimes in misdirected ways.

A second internal antidevelopment factor is neglect of agriculture. With three-fourths of the people in underdeveloped countries rural, does it make sense to neglect agriculture in order to develop industries unrelated to it? Evidence increasingly shows that it does not, a point of view that I will return to later.

A third internal factor working against development is poorly placed investments. Many countries have promoted highly mechanized, laborsaving industries, which require a great deal of scarce capital but provide relatively few jobs. In this way countries may ignore their main resource (a plentiful labor supply) and specialize in a severe shortage (capital). Poor countries have understandably invested in such industries, wanting to manufacture their own products rather than purchase from abroad, hoping that modern industrial plants would enable them to duplicate more rapidly the experience of developed countries. But industrial development that has no supporting base in grass-roots purchasing power creates a small modern sector separated from the rest of the economy. The cost of importing technology and heavy equipment for an industry may exceed the cost of importing its manufactured products. In addition these infant industries need tariff protection, but protected industries frequently remain inefficient and produce inferior goods at prices that are not competitive outside the country. Sometimes the products—plastic ware, for instance—actually throw local craftsmen out of work.

Prestige projects also illustrate misdirected investment. Newly independent nations (and sometimes new leaders) feel a particular need for symbols of nationhood and may use a high percentage of their investment capital for government buildings and monuments, or high-visibility development projects. For the same reason they often pour money into military forces. Nationalism has also fed the illusion that certain prestige industries such as auto and steel will modernize the nation.

Another internal hindrance is the growing gap between rich and poor within the underdeveloped countries. No antidevelopment factor is more obstinate, and according to the Pearson report, "Policies which serve to distribute income more equitably must therefore become as important as those designed to accelerate growth."

Unfortunately development often takes place for a small segment of the population, but leaves the great majority behind. Latin America has the most severe inequalities, despite its advantage over Asia and Africa in modern industry, and not surprisingly that area is also the most politically volatile. In its stated principles, almost every poor nation favors greater equality, and many of them talk as though this is taking place; frequently the opposite is happening. These countries lack the tradition (admittedly recent and uneven) in developed countries of moving the entire population upward with the economy; and the underdeveloped world has more people to move and fewer resources with which to move them. As the poor stay behind, the rich often fail to invest in enterprises that could generate jobs and increase productivity. They may spend their money in land speculation, ship it off to Swiss, Canadian, or U.S. banks, or use it in other ways that perpetuate a dual economy in which the rich get richer and the poor stay hungry.

Theorists have long argued that, at least in early stages of development, wealth concentrated in the hands of a few means higher savings, which can be plowed back into the economy and make it grow. The evidence, however, refutes this idea, showing that some of the countries with the most equal distribution of income are also those with the highest rates of personal savings. More important, wealthy people tend to spend their money on luxuries, which provide relatively few jobs for the general population, while poor people whose incomes are improved will spend it on food, clothes, housing, tools, bikes, and the like—things that generate employment and spread economic growth.

If internal obstacles are the responsibility of each developing country, then external obstacles are the responsibility of the already-developed nations, who show on an international scale the reluctance of a wealthy elite to sacrifice advantages. *One such external factor is international trade, as it is now practiced*—an issue I will deal with in Chapter 8.

A second external obstacle is lopsided business arrangements. When a rich man does business with a poor man, the terms of their agreement are usually weighted in the rich man's favor. The same is true among nations, as they engage in international trade and investment. Evil intent is not a prerequisite. A company with capital and development skills has no choice but to work with the ruling elite of a low-income country in order to do business; but those it must do business with often represent the antidevelopment forces of that country, standing in the way of needed reforms and of spreading economic benefits to the poor. Company officials may be unaware of this. They are oriented toward profits. Because of complications and uncertainties, they rightly expect a higher, faster return than they would get on a similar investment in their own country. The outcome, however, may militate against, rather than promote, genuine development.

Underdeveloped countries usually lack sufficient capital and management skills to develop modern industries. Even with the best of intentions, they are not in a good bargaining position and must offer generous inducements in order to attract foreign companies. But if too much profit goes back to the investing companies and if local people are not taught skills and brought into managerial positions, far from spreading economic benefits, such enterprises discourage national industries. In fact national industries sometimes sell out to foreign companies. In these ways foreign companies may come to control a nation's entire economy. When we also take into account the fact that shipping, banking, and tariff regulations, as well as the terms of trade, are dominated by the rich nations, should we be surprised that underdeveloped countries increasingly look upon international business as an extension of colonialism and are demanding an improved set of rules?

Another external factor discouraging development is the scarcity of genuine economic aid. The Decade of Development was marked, ironically, by a slowing down of economic assistance, measured as a percentage of rich nations' economic output. In addition a growing proportion of assistance took the form of loans; more loans were offered at higher rates of interest; and as the indebtedness of underdeveloped countries climbed, so did the amount of money that they returned to donor nations in the form of repayments and interest. The word "aid" is a misnomer in any case. Most of it is tied to purchases in the donor country. According to Takeshi Watanabe, former President of the Asian Development Bank, "economic aid in the form of a deferred-payment loan is nothing but an expedient to make money."

An obstacle that combines both external and internal elements is "cultural colonialism," an international version of keeping up with the Joneses. The transfer and imposition of culture is nothing new, nor is cultural spread necessarily bad; economic development

requires enormous cultural change. It is possible, however, even
with the purest of motives, to introduce ways of doing things that
work in Europe and North America, but have serious drawbacks in
a poverty-stricken society. *of cultural colonialism*

Medicine is a good example. The human compassion that spread
the practice of medicine abroad is difficult to fault. But a medical
student from an underdeveloped country who trains to practice in
the Western style expects to work in a well-equipped clinic or
hospital, and will attract patients who can afford that kind of
treatment. Instead of a handful of such physicians, what a poor
country may need more urgently are a large number of village
medical aides, trained and supervised by physicians to diagnose
common illnesses, dispense medicines, vaccinate, and help with
family planning.

Education illustrates cultural colonialism because it, too, usually
follows European and North American models. In the European
colonies education had the practical objective of preparing nationals to fill positions (largely in administration and civil service)
that would be useful in helping the Europeans run those colonies.
Thus academic courses leading to liberal arts degrees benefited a
few who became part of a well-paid Westernized local elite. Today
this type of education prepares a high number of dropouts who
consider themselves failures. Graduates often can do little that
helps development, but they expect positions and salaries appropriate to their schooling. The Pearson report says, "In too many
instances, children who finish primary school in rural areas seem
rather *less* fit to become creative and constructive members of their
own community than if they had never been to school." Each
developing country needs basic vocational and technical schools,
and adult-education programs that multiply literacy far more
rapidly than traditional primary schools do.

Consumerism provides a less benign example. U.S. citizens
spend staggering sums for nonessentials, the appetite for which
has been artificially stimulated by Madison Avenue advertising
techniques. Still, it can be argued, in a wealthy nation like ours this

kind of consumerism is not entirely wasteful. In underdeveloped countries, however, it is cruelty or madness to promote luxury products. Thirst gets translated into a need for Cokes or cocktails. The slowly emerging middle class (the new rich of those countries) is induced to buy Barbie Dolls, colored toilet paper, transistors, imported tobacco, and cosmetics. Funds desperately needed for such things as rural development, education, or labor-intensive industry instead reach a dead end; profits go outside the country or to wealthy nationals, but do not spread benefits to people who crave a decent diet.

These obstacles to development threaten to bury the underdeveloped world in a permanent sea of misery. They have to be dealt with candidly by both rich and poor nations through the adoption of positive alternatives. For this reason I will sketch an approach to development that begins where most poor people still live: on the countryside.

6

Agricultural Development

Much of the world goes hungry because farmers and farm workers are a neglected majority. Even in the United States, 40 percent of our poor live in rural areas, although only one-quarter of the population is rural. But in underdeveloped countries *three-fourths* of the population live off the land. To reverse a biblical maxim: the laborers are plentiful but the harvest is few.

A revolution of attitudes toward agriculture and changes in its practice are needed. Farmers living on a subsistence level or barely above it understandably resist change, when one miscalculation can destroy the thin security which their traditional habits insure. Paul E. Johnson, Operations Division Chief of the Office of Food for Peace, relates this experience:

When I was in Afghanistan 15 years ago, we tried to get the farmers to advance from the sickle to the scythe. A team of three Austrians worked at it for four years; a very capable young Swiss farm-tools technician with FAO spent two years on the project. After all this the Afghan farmer continued to use the sickle. Using the scythe he could cut as much wheat in an hour as he could cut with the sickle in 3 or 4, but the scythe shattered more of the grain and reduced his net yield slightly. With only an acre or two of land and with wife and children to help him in the field, labor costs were not important, but each teacup full of wheat was important in feeding hungry mouths until the next harvest.

No matter how much he may want to better himself, a farmer eking out a marginal existence cannot afford to gamble. Improvements have to be demonstrated, and must be part of an integrated program of change that offers him a social and economic security more dependable than the one he is asked to give up. The eagerness with which farmers grabbed hold of "green revolution" technologies shows, however, that given clear opportunity for improving their conditions, farmers adopt new methods as readily as anyone else.

Improvements can give a farmer pride in himself and in his vocation. As of now, most countries suffer at every level from a bias against agriculture, and ambitions are directed away from rather than toward it. Speaking about this, agriculturalist Norman Borlaug says, "The miseries of life on the land are such that once you get an education you want to become a doctor or a lawyer or professor—anything but an agricultural scientist." This attitude toward agriculture has become institutionalized by leaders in government, business, and the professions, who feel exactly the same way about farm work as the peasants do. "The agricultural adviser should be the main instigator of technical progress," according to René Dumont, a specialist in agricultural development. "But in Africa he is a comparatively underestimated official and all he wants is a position in the capital, after a period in Europe. He is not nearly so well treated as his colleagues in the Health and Education Departments." Dumont reports an experience with a Brahmin agricultural adviser in India who refused to go into the rice fields, in order to keep his shoes from getting muddy. According to a study of the educational backgrounds of the Ministers of Agriculture in Latin America, of those whose backgrounds could be determined, six were army officers, four lawyers, two doctors, and one held an undergraduate degree in animal husbandry.

Underdeveloped countries need a national goal for rural improvement and an idealism that prompts workers with a broad range of skills to go to farms and villages to involve the rural masses in economic development. This type of movement cannot take place without aggressive efforts at every level of government.

Rural development requires a labor-intensive approach in order to capitalize as much as possible on the liability of a mushrooming labor force. Modernizations which demand large capital outlays and displace labor create more problems than they solve. The combination of low yields per acre and unemployed peasants moving to urban slums is partly contradictory, since farm production could improve significantly with the investment of more labor and a relatively small infusion of capital. Of course, workers who are malnourished, or who are landless and barely paid, lack motivation and sometimes physical strength to invest more of their labor. But these problems could be tackled more successfully if they were combined with a rural development program that aimed at utilizing more fully all available labor.

Instead of importing or manufacturing tractors—with hidden costs such as repair stations, parts, fuel, and training for operators—animal traction will ordinarily be more efficient. Instead of the construction of enormous dams, farmers can frequently build smaller earth dams and dig irrigation ditches. The "new technology" for rural development in poor countries calls at first for tools that can be operated manually or by animals. Most improvements toward higher production—for example the use of fertilizer, irrigation, second-cropping, terracing, improved plowing and weeding, and harvesting higher yields—demand more labor, unless machinery displaces workers. They also require some capital, but they are primarily labor-demanding improvements.

Roads are a good example. Some small farmers lead lives of misery because they cannot get food that they produce to population centers. A primitive road—maintained with labor rather than concrete—gives a job to the man working the road, better income to the farmer, and more food for the general population.

More labor is necessary also for storage and supply centers, schools, houses, clinics, and a host of other improvements, including the development of village-style industry. Farmers can concentrate on these things during the slack season, and often receive payment in food or in fertilizer. Such an approach to agricultural development may not give the national output a sudden, dramatic boost, or provide highly visible development showcases; but it would lessen urban problems and enable hungry people to eat, work, and make solid gains that ultimately benefit everyone.

A prerequisite for rural development in many countries is land reform, without which other reforms either will not occur or will mainly benefit the privileged. A majority of farmers in these countries own no land or too little land and have neither the means nor the incentive to increase production. (You cannot think of them along the lines of the family farmer in our country, but rather of the sharecropper with a few acres and a shack.)

The situation varies from area to area. Africa, with a tradition of tribal land tenure, has comparatively little need for redistribution of land, but considerable need to prevent the further accumulation of large private holdings. In many areas there, land needs to be registered for private farming. In much of Asia and Latin America, governments could reach the majority of small cultivators, those who are not even part of the market or only marginally so, by giving them, first, a stake in the land through its redistribution and, second, the means to develop that land.

In India farms have either gotten larger through mechanization, or been carved into smaller and smaller units under the crush of population growth. Either process creates more landless workers. Their social position sinks, along with their means of support. The sharecropper ordinarily keeps only half of the harvest, although he must pay for all improvements that increase production. Nor does he have security on the land as a tenant. Since most of his profits go to the landowner and those to whom he is indebted, why should he borrow to make improvements? It is no help that money lenders charge exorbitant fees; one observer noted rates of 15 percent a week in India, and said it sometimes reaches 100 percent each week for late payments there. Many already live in constant debt, a drain on both resources and hope. Land reform measures introduced in 1972 may improve this picture for millions of Indian farmers, but as this is written, the extent of those reforms is hard to measure.

Latin America has the added problem of *latifundias:* huge estates. Wealthy landowners seldom invest their profits in rural development, and from what little the governments collect in taxes an inadequate share goes for rural development. If the forgotten principle of land reform, written into the charter of the Alliance for Progress, were practiced, governments would buy much of this misused land and sell it on generous terms to people who work the soil. Governments must then insure that, with few exceptions, payments to landowners are invested again in development.

Small farms do not always answer the need for land reform. Sometimes efficiently developed plantations can be kept intact and operated like industries. In that case the relationship of land, work, and worker could be improved in other ways—higher wages or some type of cooperative are possibilities. On the whole, however, the small farm makes sense. It provides pride, incentive, and is often the only way to bring farmers into the economy as buyers and sellers. Recent studies have shown that small private farms can increase production even more effectively than large ones, and they have the advantages of requiring less capital and being labor-intensive. Taiwan, for example, has a 7-acre limit on farms. One development specialist has pointed out:

In Taiwan, these land limitations have induced the successful farmer to be increasingly innovative with his small acreage; whereas in the Punjab, a farmer who has been successful with one innovation has tended instead to take advantage of it by buying more backward and labor-intensive farms. This means that Punjabi farms of over 100 acres have more than doubled in size on average in recent years; and, as a result, the successful farm in Taiwan is not only far more labor-intensive, but is also much more productive in terms of yields per acre.

He adds that the combination of increased yields and a labor-intensive approach has characterized economic breakthroughs in Japan, Taiwan, and South Korea.

The unplanned trend in the United States toward driving millions of farm families off the land and frequently into urban slums does not have to be copied. It has proved costly for this nation. Some consolidation was warranted, but excessive consolidation has taken place because agricultural policies, theoretically designed to help the small farmer, helped the large farm corporation much more. In addition tax laws, by permitting write-offs on purchases of land, have encouraged corporations to buy land in sizable quantities. If our country has victimized itself, impoverished countries with escalating numbers of unemployed have all the more reason to plan carefully along the lines of labor-intensive farming, with the benefits spread widely. A key to that is often land reform.

But if land reform is essential for development in so many countries, why is it seldom taking place? Because wealthy landowners and others who have a stake in maintaining their privileges resist it—imagine the reaction in our own country to a movement for chopping up Southern plantations or California agribusinesses into small family farms. Land reform found its place on the agenda of some countries, notably India, during their struggle for independence. Once the nations became independent, however, land reform took a back seat, because big landowners had extensive political leverage. Besides, those who led the struggle for independence were mostly people of means who lived in cities.

In many countries the leadership never welcomed the idea of land reform. Conservative regimes in Latin America chafed when President Kennedy had agrarian reform written into the principles of the Alliance in 1961. Not surprisingly they ignored it, and with the change in political climate during the 1960s, it dropped from the language of U.S. officials as well. Partly because it seemed a dead horse, development specialists have looked for signs of hope elsewhere—in the green revolution or in economic growth rates. But rural poverty is not so easily wished away.

In the long run land reform stabilizes a country and provides a strong antidote to violent revolution, but in the short run it creates conflict. Landowners feel threatened. Peasants become conscious that deprivation is not inevitable and determine to rise above it. This poses a dilemma for democratic governments; either the *attempt* to introduce land reform or the *failure* to introduce it could convulse a country to the left or right. Extreme polarization is by no means inevitable, however, as countries like Japan and India have shown. Following years of widespread violence by guerillas, Colombia, with a moderate, democratic government, developed a public consensus for land reform under which farms are expropriated from absentee owners and sold or awarded to tenants.

Both India and Colombia also illustrate that the redistribution of land by itself offers no panacea. Nevertheless it is an important, often crucial method in a comprehensive approach to agricultural development.

What are the consequences of slighting agriculture and neglecting rural life? Doing so hinders food production and distribution. It insures that the income gap will continue to widen in most developing countries. It stimulates migration from farms to cities, transferring unemployment and poverty to places where they are even more difficult to cope with. If the world's hungry are to eat well, and if development is to have meaning for more than a privileged minority, then the overall strategy of emphasizing agriculture makes sense.

7

Industrial Development

Industrial development moves us from the countryside to the city geographically, and unfortunately for agricultural development, the saying holds true, "Out of sight, out of mind." Yet nothing is more crucial to the cities of impoverished nations than agricultural development. The population in most of those countries is overwhelmingly rural, but becoming urbanized too rapidly. To a large extent this pull to the city, or push from the countryside, occurs *because* rural areas have been so neglected. Paradoxically, the best thing for the cities is agricultural development.

That does not mean backing away from industry, but rather *putting industry to work for agriculture, and vice versa.* In this way development spreads gains throughout the entire population.

How does a country put industry and agriculture to work for each other? Industry can concentrate on manufacturing fertilizers, tools, and other products vital to farmers for increasing their output. For example, according to one estimate, 26 million tons of fertilizer will be needed annually in underdeveloped countries by 1980. For an overall investment of $4 billion, about $3 billion (or 20 million tons) of fertilizer could be produced each year in those countries, representing some sizable industries, and even more sizable gains in terms of agricultural development. That would be true, however, only within the context of an overall farm program, including distribution, marketing, and loans to indigent farmers for purchases. It would not succeed if a government allowed wealthier farmers to gobble up more land, or to bring in laborsaving machines at will, and left small farmers without the means of buying fertilizer and high-yield seeds. If that happens, marginal farmers will be knocked out of competition and driven to the cities even faster, and industry will not be serving agriculture—or itself in the long run.

A country can also achieve integrated growth by developing other industries that are closely related to agriculture. Poor countries can learn from the period of the Industrial Revolution, when industry relied extensively on agricultural growth for its impetus, and in turn fed that growth. The mining of iron ore, for example, supplied raw material for farm tools and machines. The textile industry made finished products from cotton, wool, and other fibers. Exports should be planned with the same close relationship in mind, so that the productive capacity of the land is fully exploited, and emphasis laid on shipping abroad manufactured goods rather than raw materials. In this way rural development and manufacturing for export can move ahead together.

The experience of the West during the Industrial Revolution deserves emphasis. It is ironic that people in the underdeveloped countries who want to copy Western industrial patterns tend to downgrade agriculture, overlooking the fact that integration of industry and agriculture was central to development in the West. Initial stages of industrial growth in Europe and North America depended upon earlier agricultural development, and as farmers became consumers, they helped to spawn industries not directly related to agriculture. Today, as well, countries need agricultural development as a base for industrial growth.

Industries that have no close connection with agriculture may also be vital to a country's economy. Zambia, with four million people, is the world's third largest copper producer, but the wealth brought by the mines has created a giant wage gap between mine workers and rural peasants. A national resource like copper needs to benefit the rural population, too, but that can only happen if the profits of this industry are spread more evenly in the form of rural development.

Without a more even spread of economic advantages, poverty-stricken farm families will be pushed or pulled prematurely in greater numbers to urban centers, seeking nonexistent or marginal jobs.

Social scientist Albert Meister gives us a composite view of the landless peasant family of Latin America that migrates to the city. Unprepared for the crisis that will tear it apart, the family arrives virtually destitute at a shantytown near the edge of a city and assembles a makeshift shelter. Members of the family—stable, orderly, honest, and with respect for the traditional role of the father and mother—cling tenaciously to one another and to the values they brought with them. Then the crisis unfolds. The man cannot find steady work; he feels overwhelmed by the impersonality and confusion of the city. As their economic situation deteriorates, he loses self-respect, and the others grow discouraged. Fearful, emotionally isolated, and yearning for their soil, they finally get swallowed up by their shantytown surroundings. The man turns to alcohol and extramarital relations. The children get into fights, quit school, and feel deserted by their parents, especially their father, which may literally be the case. Chaos replaces order in the shack, as it has already done in their lives.

The family may pass through this crisis. If so, the father, or perhaps now a common-law husband, finds work and the family begins to save for the day when it can move out of the shantytown. The children find more ordered lives again. But progress is fragile, so an injury, an illness, or the loss of a job can precipitate another crisis, from which the family may not recover. Or the family may not recover from the first crisis. In either case, if the man becomes alcoholic and the wife is forced to work or depend on a succession of partners, the children may turn to crime and prostitution. So far a majority of rural migrants eventually make it past the shanty-town, says Meister, but the economic facts of life in most Latin American countries increasingly work against doing so.

The New York Times cites the spread of shantytowns in Afri-can cities, where factories—because they are so few—offer "scant industrial opportunity for the man whose education has taught him to be dissatisfied with the primitive village life." That was in 1971, when a study showed that each year 50,000 Zambian seventh graders leave school looking for work, although the entire economy of Zambia has only 350,000 paying jobs. Many young men wind up selling bits of stolen merchandise on the streets, the crime rate growing with unemployment. Nigeria began executing thieves publicly because armed robbery became so prevalent, but with Lagos, the capitol, increasing by more than 10 percent a year and joblessness rampant, the move hardly provided a solution. African cities are doubling every decade at the present rate. Before World War II, tropical Africa had five cities over 100,000; now it has 60.

Unlike the earlier experience of Europe and North America, migration to the cities in underdeveloped countries is much larger and occurs far ahead of industrial growth. To find something like it in the United States you turn to the migration from the rural South of several million impoverished blacks, who arrived in the cities when unskilled hands were no longer in demand. Because our situation has never been honestly faced, it has generated diffi-culties far out of proportion to the original problem. Still, it is microscopic compared to the migration now going on in the underdeveloped countries.

In those countries the already massive labor force is multiplying annually by 2.5 to 3 percent, a rate roughly five times faster than that which today's rich countries usually experienced when they were at comparable stages of development. In India alone perhaps 10,000 more people join the ranks of the unemployed every day, some of them engineers and college graduates; and like most poor countries, India offers no unemployment compensation. Even with improved industrial growth, unemployment seems certain to climb sharply, as the population expansion of the 1950s and 1960s floods the labor market. Once again the underdeveloped countries are "getting there too late," because they need industry for jobs at a time when industry gears toward high-cost, laborsaving technology.

Mounting unemployment underscores a second major requirement: the need for *labor-intensive* industries. One method that fits well with an emphasis on agriculture, and encourages a more even distribution of the population, is the development of small industries in rural towns and villages. These industries can turn out clothing, furniture, simple tools, and products of various handicrafts, using mainly local materials and locally developed skills. The goods can often be marketed locally as well.

Large industries are also necessary, and underdeveloped countries may be so desperate for them that they (1) spend most of their development funds on this sector, and (2) persuade, by whatever means necessary, foreign investors to establish industries. If those industries promise relatively few jobs for the capital invested, host countries may feel that a few jobs are better than none, or be lured by the hope—often disappointed—of earning much foreign exchange. Facing massive poverty and unemployment with few resources puts great pressure on poor countries to gamble on this approach. Yet their needs dictate not only greater emphasis on the rural sector, but industries that provide as many jobs as possible.

This dilemma for the underdeveloped countries underscores the potential contribution of multinational corporations, which in recent years have rapidly accelerated the practice of taking capital and technology to those countries for the advantage of their cheap labor and raw materials. This has in many instances rationalized production across national lines to the benefit of everyone. But it can carry heavy liabilities. Poor countries may offer such firms low interest loans, overvalued exchange rates, or special tax breaks. These amount to expensive subsidies. If in addition the industries are capital-intensive, poor countries may find themselves creating jobs at an unrealistic cost per job.

These dangers can be avoided by policies which make it more costly for companies to use capital-intensive technology, and which offer advantages instead of methods that are labor-intensive. Taiwan and South Korea did this so successfully that by 1970 they had cut back unemployment dramatically and were together exporting almost three times as much in manufactured goods as all of Latin America, even though Latin American industrial capacity is eight times greater. Of course, Taiwan and South Korea had the advantages of massive economic assistance and a relatively well-educated population.

Experiences of the past decade, then, suggest integrating industrial development with agricultural development, and favoring labor-intensive technologies for both.

8

Trade

In the last two chapters I sketched a way out of hunger and poverty unified around agriculture and postulated on a number of reforms. It may sound simple on paper. In reality the way out is exceedingly difficult. It can only work if heroic efforts by the underdeveloped countries are combined with expanding opportunities for equitable trade and greater economic asistance, both of which depend on a generous response from the rich nations.

Trade, not aid, is by far the most important type of economic transaction between rich and poor nations. It is unfortunate that while the volume of exports has increased for the poor nations, their *share* in world exports shrank from 31 percent in 1950 to 17 percent in 1971. Underdeveloped countries pay, by their own exports, for the vast majority of imports which are vital to their economic growth. The Pearson commission observed that "growth rates of individual developing countries since 1950 correlate better with their export performance than with any other single economic indicator." So crucial is trade to those countries that aid, by comparison, has been called a "soft option."

Lester B. Pearson, the late Canadian Prime Minister, once related to a UN official the pressure on a government to prefer that soft option:

You sit at the Cabinet table [he said in effect] and you tell your colleagues that country X, which we have helped before, has asked for another $Y million. The Minister of Finance, to whom you appeal, agrees that he might perhaps be able to oblige with the necessary funds, but the Minister of Trade intervenes and asks whether it would not be more helpful to assist the exports of country X by allowing duty free entry to Z million shirts. There is an immediate protest from the Minister of Labour, who foresees trouble. You hesitate, and, in the end, you settle for the softer option. You give country X another $Y million, not forgetting that it used some of the previous aid funds to establish a shirt factory for the export trade.

Pearson's example illustrates how poor countries get locked into a losing arrangement. The rules for losing include these five steps:

First, raw materials and primary products have low commercial value and account for almost 90 percent of the export earnings of underdeveloped countries. With these low-cost materials, companies in the rich nations manufacture high-value products—which account for *almost all* of their exports to the underdeveloped countries. In 1971 poor nations suffered a $2.6 billion loss in balance of trade; but discounting the oil-rich countries, the trade-balance deficit that year for the poor nations stood at *$11.5 billion.*

Second, terms of trade (the relationship of export to import prices) have turned against the poor nations over the past two decades, as prices progressively dropped for the raw materials and primary products they sell, in relation to the manufactured products and advanced technology they have to buy from rich nations. Despite a stabilizing trend in the 1960s, the Secretariat of the UN Conference on Trade and Development has estimated that worsening terms of trade cost the poor nations $2.5 billion each year. Such losses constitute a huge subsidy to the rich nations.

Third, many poor countries find themselves dependent for export earnings on a single crop, such as bananas, coffee, or sugar.

The market tends to be low and fluctuates greatly. When I asked the president of one Central American country what his chances of staying in power were, in view of the obvious turmoil in that country, he responded, "It depends on the price of coffee." He turned out to be a good prophet. The price of coffee went down, turmoil increased, and he was assassinated.

Fourth, tariffs and quotas often prevent underdeveloped countries from exporting manufactured goods. In the major trade negotiations of the 1960s (the Kennedy Round) rich nations helped one another by lowering import barriers on products that they manufacture and sell to one another, but largely bypassed farm commodities and the type of labor-intensive goods manufactured by poor nations. As James P. Grant, President of the Overseas Development Council has stressed, "the tariff structure in force today in the developed countries leads them in effect to charge twice as much duty on the goods they import from the developing world than on the goods they import from one another." For example, U.S. tariffs escalate so that they are lowest on raw materials, higher on semiprocessed imports, and highest on finished products. But this turns reason inside-out. Poor countries need most of all encouragement to *process* raw materials and *manufacture* products. Otherwise they are doomed to perpetual subservience: using their raw materials for the rich nations, who reap most of the profits.

Fifth, rich nations have agricultural export policies which are costly to their own people, and discourage the development of a healthy agricultural base in developing countries. In the European Common Market cereal prices almost double world market prices. Japan subsidizes rice production at nearly three times the world market price. The United States protects domestic production of beet sugar, although tropical cane sugar is both superior and far less expensive. Rich nations give approximately four times as much aid to their own farmers as they do to all of the underdeveloped countries combined. In the United States a disproportionate amount of that aid goes to farm corporations, reflecting a tendency for agricultural policies to make the rich richer.

If developed nations hold all the advantages, including terms of trade unfavorable to the poor countries, then the market is not free. It is rigged. But neither is the market free if tariffs are simply equalized or removed on both sides, because the countries do not do business as equals. Naked free trade will continue to hand rich countries advantages, although it remains the goal for trading equals. The only way to make arrangements fair is to turn the tables temporarily and establish trade policies that deliberately favor the developing countries. In 1971 and 1972 most of the noncommunist aid-giving countries (but not the United States) put tariff preferences into effect. These are hedged in, however, by a variety of quotas, excluded products, and in the case of the Common Market countries, special access for them (through tariff concessions) to underdeveloped markets, which really need protection. The result is to nullify much of the value of those preferences.

In some cases international agreements on prices and production can also give underdeveloped countries a fairer chance. According to historian J. H. Parry, the Virginia colony was saved from economic ruin and allowed to achieve modest wealth when England agreed to destroy its own tobacco acreage and give the Virginia planters a monopoly on this crop. In the same spirit, adjustments on the part of rich nations today could help to achieve long-range benefits for everyone.

Stability in trade arrangements is also essential. Poor nations must know that if they develop a successful industry it will not be put out of business with one stroke of a pen by the President of the United States through an arbitrary shift in tariffs or quotas. Uncertainty about U.S. trade policies often discourages those with wealth in underdeveloped countries from investing in domestic enterprises. If you had $500,000 and you lived in one of the developing countries, would you invest it there or put the money in a Swiss or North American bank? Frequently we encourage the wrong answer.

Part of the solution to trade problems is for poor nations to expand trade among themselves. *As of now trade between underdeveloped countries—two-thirds of the world—amounts to less than 4 percent of all world trade.* Expansion could be facilitated through common markets or other regional agreements, but so far only a few serious attempts have been made. Why? One reason is that many countries are newly independent and have enough difficulty securing their own national loyalties, without the complication of establishing regional ties as well. In addition the transportation routes and industries of many of the countries were built up to forge links not with their neighbors, but with their European colonizers. Most of all, the need to sell where there is purchasing power, and heavy reliance on industrialized countries for aid, investment, and technology prompt poor nations to emphasize trade with the rich ones.

Trade expansion between poor countries depends to a large extent on their own economic development, which in turn, ironically, depends on better access to markets in the rich countries. That access will require internal adjustments on the part of the rich nations—a problem I take up in Chapter 13—but these adjustments are modest problems compared to what is at stake for poor countries.

Tariffs and quotas cannot be dropped overnight, and preferences granted at once to underdeveloped countries. But we can move steadily in that direction.

9

Economic Assistance

Before long the poor countries may literally be giving economic aid to the rich ones. Many argue that this already takes place through transfers of raw material and manufactured goods, though not yet in money flows. In 1971 the overall balance of payments (which includes trade and investment flows) for the underdeveloped countries gave them a surplus of $3.5 billion—but only $1.1 billion excluding the oil-producing countries. According to the 1972 annual report of the World Bank, the net gain in official and officially guaranteed loans and grants (new loans and grants minus repayments) from rich nations rose marginally from $4.9 billion in 1965 to $5.3 billion in 1970, but in real value those transfers declined about 10 to 15 percent because of rising costs for goods and services. In addition population growth decreased the *per capita* value to recipient nations another 13 percent. The direction of aid is downward.

As public debts soar for the underdeveloped countries—the 1961 figure of $21 billion had quadrupled by 1973—repayments also rise: they were $4 billion in

1967, $6 billion in 1970. The amount of money these countries return each year to the rich nations, measured as a percentage of new loans and grants received, is increasing: 41 percent in 1967, and 53 percent in 1970. A continuation of this trend would obviously compel poor nations to aid the rich ones before long. And if other investment and trade flows are also considered, as they should be, that point could arrive within a few years. Or rich nations could hasten it by following the example of the United States in cutting economic assistance.

If such a reversal of financial flows occurs, it could mark the collapse of development hopes for much of the world. It is hard to imagine the peace and economic stability of our own country not ultimately threatened by this topsy-turvy prospect of poor nations contributing to the rich.

Because development has to be accomplished basically through self-help, I want to emphasize that only a small part of new investment in the underdeveloped countries comes from the rich nations. About 85 percent comes from their own savings, and the remainder consists mainly of private foreign investment, and loans rather than grants. The significant fact, however, is that generous financing from an outside government has almost always been crucial to *fast* growth, and speed is essential because development has to catch up with runaway population. Apart from a few oil-rich countries, the only rapidly developing noncommunist nations are those that have received extraordinary assistance.

Although development depends mainly on each country using its own resources, chiefly abundant labor, we cannot escape the fact that even a labor-intensive approach requires money in substantial amounts; yet so far the rich nations have given little financial backing to labor-intensive development programs. Take rural development as an example. A simple thing like the use of fertilizer means that poor farmers need access to credit at low rates of interest, and that presupposes a reserve of capital. It may also suggest the desirability of establishing a fertilizer industry, but that, too, has to be financed. When you add the cost of other improvements such as pest control, equipment, and building materials, the importance of capital becomes obvious. Determination and muscle are not enough. Furthermore grass-roots leaders should spread throughout the countryside and work with the rural population in teaching a wide variety of skills. The cost of this may be modest in terms of eventual returns, but the cost cannot be wished away. The same applies to redistribution of land.

Food-for-work projects provide another example of labor-intensive development, but they, too, require capital in the form of food and in the nonlabor costs of construction. Food-for-work projects involve primarily public works such as roads, clinics, schools, electrification, and irrigation canals. Farmers can undertake these projects during the months when they are not occupied with farming. Better nourishment is an important objective of these programs. The need of farmers for food may sound ludicrous to us, but most of the hungry people of the world live off the land. Approximately three-fourths of the farmers in India do not have any food to sell. Agriculturalist René Dumont says of a particular area in India that, with extra food rations to give them needed energy, workers could have dredged irrigation reservoirs during the off season and prepared rich fields that would have produced two harvests instead of one each year.

The World Food Program of the United Nations sponsors food-for-work projects, but it operates with approximately $130 million a year, "a pathetically inadequate multilateral response to the vast and growing needs of millions of malnourished and underemployed human beings," according to its Director, Francisco Aquino. The state of Illinois receives much more than that—$174 million—in a single year from its cigarette tax. Multiplying food-for-work money would enable additional millions to engage in rural development. Rather than "dumping" food on the market (a practice that hurts farmers and destroys incentive for increasing food production), food-for-work supplements diets of those who are marginally nourished. This program offers one way of expanding food markets for both developed and underdeveloped countries. Its underfunding illustrates the human waste in our pinch-penny approach to economic assistance.

A research gap also illustrates the timid supply of assistance. Our prosperous third of the world uses 87 percent of the world's output, but it does almost *all* of the research. The two-thirds of humanity most in need of new techniques and inventions cannot afford to divert their meager savings for that purpose. Assistance for research is needed to fill an enormous void. The outstanding example is sponsorship by the Rockefeller and Ford Foundations of agricultural institutes, which spurred the green revolution in wheat and rice and are engaged at an earlier stage of research on production of tropical foods. Although higher yield crops in the tropics and subtropics are a matter of utmost urgency, major research centers in those regions are new and few. Because conditions vary so greatly, such research needs to be carried on intensively in virtually every country.

Results of research in developed nations often can be used to great advantage in the underdeveloped countries. But that advantage carries with it the risk of getting caught in a "technology trap," because poor countries, having little alternative, may adopt technologies that are not suited to their conditions. For example, research and development on farm machinery and industrial equipment in our country moves us toward more sophisticated automation—about the last thing poor countries need. They should, as a rule, be finding a more "primitive" technology that makes use of abundant workers, not one that displaces them. According to agricultural economist Carl K. Eicher, "The design of mechanical technology so as to complement labour use, rather than substitute for it, is a high-priority area of research in Africa in the 1970s." But it is hardly being touched.

I am stressing farm technology here, but similar examples could be mentioned in a wide range of areas. Ivan Illich of the Center for Intercultural Documentation in Cuernavaca, Mexico, has called for "counterfoil" research which would aim at alternatives to basic products and services which now bypass the poor. Many imaginative alternatives are needed and much of the impetus for this research, partly in manpower but especially in funding, will have to come from the rich nations.

These illustrations indicate why the crucial difference between stagnation and momentum can be provided by economic assistance. It is therefore a matter of grave consequence that, measured as a percentage of rich countries' national output, as well as in value to the poor countries, official development assistance has steadily dropped for more than a decade. Furthermore the trend of that assistance has been away from grants and toward high-interest loans. But this paves the way for the rich nations to become net recipients of money from the poor ones, a scrooge-like arrangement that ignores the benefit that development could confer on the entire world.

10

Models of Development

Attempts at development show wide-spread diversity. No two countries are alike, and the great majority of new nations avoid lining up in the camp of either communist-type socialism or unrestrained capitalism. They are trying to find their own paths in ways that subordinate economic theories to practical considerations. With diversity the rule, and bearing in mind that no "pure" models exist, one may for convenience designate countries as having capitalist, hard-line socialist, or mixed economies.

CAPITALIST MODELS | *Japan* stands high as the success story of Asia, although its value as a model to underdeveloped countries is limited by a few unusual advantages. As a northern country, Japan enjoys a nontropical climate. It moved toward industrialization rapidly in the late nineteenth century and emerged strong enough by 1941 to launch a war against the United States and conquer most of Southeast Asia. It became a rich, developed nation while most of today's poor nations were still colonies, and now ranks behind only the United States and Russia in total output. (Some experts predict that within two decades Japan will become, per capita, the wealthiest country in the world.) Japan's insularity encouraged social cohesion, and spared it the trauma of being reduced to a European colony. Starting in the late nineteenth century, Japanese governments imposed drastic reforms by authoritarian rule in order to prepare for industrialization.

More changes under the U.S. occupation followed the Japanese surrender. A land-reform measure, for example, compelled absentee landowners to sell most of their land to the government, which then resold it to tenant farmers on easy terms. It also restricted the number of acres a single farmer could own. Since at the time half the population was rural, compared to about one-fourth now, that allowed industry time to develop a need for more workers and paved the way for migration to the cities. Because Japan's natural resources are severely limited natural resources, it imports raw materials in abundance. These it turns into profitable manufactured goods. After World War II the Allied command also began dissolving huge family combines that controlled Japan's industry, but dropped that reform in the hope of strengthening Japan economically.

To the envy of many, Japan has achieved a kind of national partnership—a benevolent capitalistic version of central planning —in which government, banking, industry, and labor work together with a remarkable sense of harmony. Diligence, respect for authority, and a literacy rate higher than our own characterize the Japanese people and indicate some of Japan's advantages. Young people, however, are increasingly challenging the nation's inclination to measure progress in terms of higher production and incomes.

Kenya in East Africa stands out as a nation that is making economic gains by encouraging private enterprise, including foreign investment. Since 1964, the first full year of Kenya's independence, its economic growth rate has averaged more than 6 percent a year. That gives 12 million Kenyans a per capita annual income of about $155. No private industries have been national-ized, but the government keeps private ownership diffused in order to prevent a concentration of economic power. Kenya seeks foreign investors, and offers loans and other incentives to local entrepre-neurs who can develop a business or industry; but it insists that these harmonize with Kenya's development goals. The state also exercises some control over wages and prices. In these respects private enterprise is not free to do as it pleases.

The Kenyan government speaks of "African socialism," but spells this out in terms of familiar equalitarian ideals, with a stress on "mutual social responsibility." According to one government booklet, "The State has an obligation to ensure equal opportunities . . . and provide needed social services such as education, medi-cal care and social security." The government points out that the traditional tribal view of property emphasizes its use for the general welfare much more than the Western legal idea of abso-lute property rights for the individual. In practice, however, Kenya moves toward the Western definition in such acts as registering defined pieces of farmland to squatters.

Kenya's five-year plan for 1970–74 aims at a more even distri-bution of incomes through graduated income taxes that exempt those with "average" or below-average incomes, through wage and price controls, and through free or inexpensive health and educa-tion services for the poor. While Kenya is making efforts to carry out its income-distribution policy, that goal is badly undermined by rising unemployment. With an annual population growth rate above 3 percent, and almost half of Kenya's population below the age of fifteen, unemployment seems certain to get worse. In July, 1970, the government ordered all employers to hire an additional 10 percent of workers. A news service wirephoto showed thou-sands of young men lined up to apply for jobs. But of the 230,000 who applied, only 36,000 got jobs, many of which turned out to be temporary. In 1971, 160,000 Kenyans graduated from primary schools, but barely a third of them continued in school or found jobs.

Kenya faces this mounting problem by making rural development the fundamental strategy of its latest five-year plan, since almost 90 percent of the population lives off the land. Until recently rural development funds were used primarily for re-settling Africans on several million acres of choice farmland previously held by Europeans. (Some farmland and most of the plantations and ranches are still owned by Europeans, but by 1969, 47,000 African families were farming land previously owned by 2,000 Europeans.) Now the emphasis has shifted to improved farming methods and various rural projects. But lack of credit for poor farmers remains "an important constraint on agricultural development," according to the five-year plan. At another level, Kenya's Protestant churches and several government ministries have started seven "village polytechnics" for training young people in a variety of vocational skills needed on farms and in villages. The government admits that even with successful rural development programs, migration to towns and cities will rise "at an exceedingly rapid rate."

Kenya pursues a policy of gradually replacing foreigners who occupy technical or managerial positions with Kenyans, and has used the threat of nationalization to insure compliance. The government has also denied licenses to thousands of East Indians who had a near-monopoly on small family-type businesses prior to independence. But this policy of "Kenyanization" provides only marginal help in slowing down the unemployment boom.

Like most underdeveloped countries, Kenya faces progressively worsening terms of trade each year. The present five-year plan acknowledges that imports will continue to rise much faster than exports. Kenya induces more private foreign investment to help pay for the difference, although by making capital cheap, relative to labor, this policy subsidizes the urban sector and conflicts with employment and rural development goals. Kenya also resorts to additional borrowing, at the risk of long-range debt-servicing problems.

Brazil, the giant of Latin America, will be closely watched to see if it is producing a development miracle or a colossal failure. *The Wall Street Journal* put its finger on Brazil's dilemma. In the first of two articles it told how Brazil's economy had gone "from mess to miracle," including a phenomenal growth rate of more than 11 percent in 1971, and an average of almost 10 percent for four consecutive years. When the military seized power in 1964, the new rulers decided to slow down gradually a soaring rate of inflation, while spurring growth. They did so primarily by absorbing excess money through the collection of more taxes. Then they offered sizable tax incentives to industries that invested in the poverty-ridden northeast, in the Amazon region, or in production for export. Spurring exports has the purpose of earning foreign exchange, so Brazil can meet payments on $6 billion in foreign debts that are falling due. Export incentives also encourage capital-intensive industries such as automobiles and precision instruments. While the country is gambling heavily on its own private industry, it has opened the door as well to foreign investors who are pouring money into Brazil (according to *The New York Times,* $3 billion in 1972, a year in which that country's GNP growth rate again climbed above 10 percent). All of this has, since 1967, made Brazil a "turnabout nation."

The second article told a strikingly different story. The economic boom, it said, "has had practically no impact at all on well over half the country's 95 million citizens. In fact, millions are actually poorer now than they were five years ago." New industries usually need skilled workers, and the modernizing of established industries often replaces workers with machines. The top 1 percent of the population earns 30 percent of the country's income. Brazil's Minister of Finance says candidly that only 5 percent of the population has benefited from five years of unprecedented growth. A U.S. State Department report estimates that real wages for two-thirds of Brazil's workers have probably been decreasing for five years. The unemployed, of course, do even worse.

In the impoverished northeast, where disease, mental retardation, and early death from malnutrition are widespread, industries have sprung up in response to government inducements. But some of these industries operate at a fraction of capacity, because so few people in the northeast have money to buy products. Industrialization and underdevelopment flourish side by side. As a result, the government has changed its policy to emphasize agricultural development (through tax incentives) in that region. Many hope that the Amazon highway will bring economic gains to the northeast; others predict that cleared jungle areas will turn into desert. Meanwhile, the one thing that Brazil's economic miracle has not yet been able to do is to spread the benefits of development to the majority of the population. They still go hungry and die early. /

HARD-LINE
SOCIALIST
MODELS

Karl Marx spun out his theory of socialism in and for an urban, industrial society, and the Soviet Union's application of that theory to agriculture has been contrived. No matter how poor, farmers were either considered capitalists because they owned the means of production, or despised for being capitalist-prone. Theory, of course, may have reinforced an existing prejudice.

China has tried to avoid the mistakes of the Russians, and although its experience, too, has been uneven, Chinese communists respect the peasantry and cultivate a sense of unity between city and countryside. This includes the compulsory movement of many young urban workers, as well as skilled professionals, to rural collectives, and medical care for the peasants through the use of para-professional "barefoot doctors." It also includes the establishment of industries in rural areas. The most striking lesson in China's economic development has to do with its attitude toward agriculture and the rural population, which accounts for 85 percent of the Chinese.

During the 1950s China concentrated mainly on building modern industry. Millions of people who streamed to the cities failed to find employment or housing—a familiar story. The Great Leap Forward, announced in 1958, put everyone to work; but critical food shortages and serious economic reversals followed. In a major policy switch China then decided to wrap its development efforts around agriculture and allied industries. By the middle 1960s economic recovery had clearly taken place. Now 800 million Chinese, with an annual per capita income averaging perhaps $140, are moving toward development unassisted.

Our knowledge of China is much too limited, but visits by specialists since 1971 reveal some surprisingly impressive gains. *Life* correspondent John Saar noted a level of overall poverty but saw "no hunger, no untreated sick, no beggars"—an observation verified by others. Gone, too, are the prostitutes and opium smokers. Swollen eyes and open skin sores no longer plague the peasants. City streets and villages are immaculate. Unemployment has been eliminated, and although wages are meager, everyone is assured housing, education, medical care, and food. As reported today—and some caution is needed because of limitations placed on visitors—China gives a picture of people moving with a sense of dignity and purpose in a setting of austerity.

Even a certain compassion comes through. René Dumont contrasts the present regime with previous ruling classes who accepted famine as nature's way of cutting down the surplus population and who ridiculed missionaries for efforts to help starving people. In 1959, when Mao's Great Leap Forward put the country on the verge of famine, the government "gritted its teeth and met scarcity with the cry 'Let no one die of hunger.' (By contrast, in the winter of 1965–66, the starving people living in the streets of New Delhi could see rich Indians coming out of gargantuan feasts.)" One observer notes that peasants in China have the equivalent of "an insurance policy against pestilence, famine, and other disasters. In this respect, China has out-performed every underdeveloped country in the world; . . ." The world has never before witnessed an attempt on such a scale to build a new society from the bottom up. Can we blame people in underdeveloped countries for watching China with keen interest?

The negative side of China's experiment shows a passionate totalitarianism that harbors little dissent. Commercial advertising is unknown, but government propaganda is everywhere. Workers' salaries are partly determined by the rating they get (from fellow workers) for political attitudes. With a highly centralized, authoritarian government, China has the ability to industrialize with some speed through "forced savings"—in a manner not altogether unlike that of the capitalists of the Industrial Revolution in the nineteenth and early twentieth centuries, who extracted enormous profits from the sweat of the workers, profits which they kept investing in more industrial expansion. Even so, this kind of go-it-alone development presupposes mineral resources needed for industrialization, and a great variety of skilled technologists—conditions few other countries enjoy.

The Chinese model is one of repulsion-attraction to the rest of the underdeveloped world. Its harsh regimentation repels, but then the Chinese have to arrange life with perhaps one-thirtieth of the per capita wealth which we enjoy; and hungry people around the world, whose lives are extensively regimented anyway, may not be so repelled if nothing else seems to offer them hope. The repulsion-attraction quality of China was underscored by Cardinal Thomas Cooray of Ceylon at the 1970 Asian bishops' conference. In calling for alternatives he said, "The tragedy of our people is that no one else other than Mao's China seems to offer realistic solutions that are radical enough to meet the urgent and grave needs of the poor Asian masses." China remains a model of last resort. Nevertheless success in moving all its people toward an adequate standard of living, along with Japan's earlier and more advanced achievement, raises this disturbing question: for how many countries will authoritarian rule seem to be the only means of bringing about reforms essential for development?

China takes its self-declared role as a model for underdeveloped countries seriously. In the mid-1960s China's efforts to stir up revolts abroad met with humiliating defeats and cost China diplomatic standing in a number of countries. After a period of withdrawal, China has taken the diplomatic initiative again, this time with considerable prestige and a more friendly face. It has dramatized its bid for recognition as the avant-garde of poor nations by underwriting the $400 million Tanzania-Zambia railway. Not incidentally, part of the showcase is the simple, frugal living habits of the thousands of Chinese technicians, qualities that the Africans find attractive compared to the extravagance of most experts from the rich nations. This kind of effort lends credibility to China's claims—just as its unyielding opposition to Bangladesh undermined that credibility. In the long run China's most important contribution to the poor countries could prove to be in research and technology, which are deliberately geared to conditions of underdevelopment.

Cuba, the Latin American version of communism, has more per capita income than China, but could fall behind in the long run. Cuba has emphasized the "health, education and welfare" part of the economy, and wiped out unemployment. It has lifted many of its people, especially farm workers, out of dismal poverty, and won popular support for the government. But consumer goods, as well as most foods, are severely rationed, and worker absenteeism runs high. Premier Castro has complained about that and about shoddy workmanship. The school dropout-truancy rate reportedly has reached 25 percent. These are problems unheard of in China. With limited natural resources, Cuba suffers further from having a one-crop economy (sugar) and great indebtedness to the Soviet Union, which aids Cuba with approximately $500 million annually.

"MIXED"   *Chile* is a comparatively prosperous Latin American
MODELS   country with an annual per capita income of about
$700, a figure that obscures its jagged distribution
of wealth. In his successful bid for the presidency in late 1970,
Marxist candidate Salvador Allende could appeal to widespread
unemployment and to the fact that 43 percent of the population
was badly nourished. An annual population growth rate of 3.2
percent and an inflation rate that reached 35 percent in 1970
spelled additional trouble for reform-minded Christian Democrats,
whose leader, Eduardo Frei, was not eligible for reelection.

Allende's program calls for the development of a "socialist and
pluralistic society"—one that will move gradually toward a socialist economy, using the framework of Chile's parliamentary
democracy with its opposition parties and free elections. Allende,
who emphasizes that he is a Marxist socialist, not a communist,
expresses pride in this democratic tradition and has said that his
government will not imitate the "centralism" of Russia, China, or
Cuba. There are different roads to socialism, and Chile will look
for its own way, according to Allende.

Since Chile's population is 70 percent urban, the government's
approach emphasizes industry, although it has included the seizure
of large farms for development of cooperatives. The government
has outlined three areas of business ownership: state, private, and
mixed, with the state area as "the prevailing one." According to
the Banco Central de Chile, state ownership will include "large
domestic and foreign monopolies, banking, foreign commerce and
the fields that have strategic importance in the nation's development." Nationalization of its U.S.-owned copper industry, ap-
proved unanimously by Chile's Senate, had also been in the
platform of the moderate Christian Democrats. The vote for
nationalization illustrates that Allende lacks a legislative majority
and must win support from the opposition for his programs.
Allende says foreign investments are still welcome. According to
the Banco Central, "the government intends to authorize those that
bring a real technological contribution to the national economy, in

any case preferring an investment in a mixed form with state capital controlling the majority of the shares."

The success of Chile's experiment will depend primarily on the government's ability to produce practical economic gains for the population, and that requires more initiative by workers as well as the dedication of those at the managerial level. Economic theory is not enough.

During 1971 Allende's administration cut unemployment in half, redistributed income through taxes and wage-price controls, and increased Chile's output by 8 percent. But lagging copper production together with low foreign-market prices for copper, a rising federal deficit, and too much consumer buying spurred a new inflationary trend in 1972, which wiped out most of Chile's reserves in foreign exchange. Food production fell behind, making more food imports necessary, as a result of disruptions that accompanied land expropriation. By late 1972 the picture was one of achievements and problems, with the long-range outcome of Allende's economic mixture uncertain.

India, another example of a mixed economy, has urban unemployment that is expected to exceed 50 million by 1980—one sample of the burdens this nation bears. In 1959 I had the opportunity to spend part of an evening with the late Prime Minister Nehru and his daughter, Indira Gandhi, who is now Prime Minister. I left the Prime Minister's residence feeling overwhelmed by the immensity of the problems which leaders there face. I remember telling a friend the next day, "If the President of the United States thinks he has problems, he should serve as Prime Minister of India for a few weeks." Making a significant dent in urban unemployment alone would require an enormous program of public works and investment in industry. But three-fourths of India's population is rural and needs by far the biggest share of economic development. *Yet the entire annual budget for this nation, which has more people than the population of Africa and South America combined, is smaller than the budget of New York*

City. Despite its need, India ranks among the lowest underdeveloped countries in per capita economic assistance.

India has primarily a free-enterprise economy, even though the government likes to talk about "our socialist pattern of society" and emerged at independence in 1947 with a bias against private investment. Agriculture—and consequently most of India—is excluded from any type of state ownership. Land reform, largely ineffectual until 1972, far from threatening free enterprise, extends it to those who did not previously participate in the system. Small-scale business and industry, a major portion of the Indian economy, is left to the private sector. Communications, transportation, banking, utilities, insurance, and a few big industries are government owned; but in practice the government mainly takes over what private enterprise is not able or willing to do. In 1972 the government announced moves toward increasing state control of basic industries, a policy that for practical reasons is not always applied.

In banking policies the government has primarily assisted the private sector; and when Prime Minister Indira Gandhi announced in 1971 the nationalization of commercial banks, she said that its purpose was to make loans available to peasants and small industries—that is, to spur private enterprise for them.

After her election in 1972, Mrs. Gandhi proposed a budget that hit the upper income levels with stiffer taxes, but avoided discouraging industry from expanding. And India continues to woo foreign investors. In a trip to New York in 1971, one of India's top investment planners pointed out that U.S. manufacturers in India earned at a rate of 14.7 percent in 1969. India is willing to gamble on a lot of profit leaving the country in order to expand industry.

To the extent that the state owns or regulates industries, it has opened itself to the charge of protecting inefficient, parasitic industries that do not have to compete in the market place. Some have, in fact, devoured a sizable but undetected government subsidy. On the other hand the government, whose management record has improved, points to benefits that do not show up on the balance sheet. These include improved housing for workers in government-run enterprises.

India's first three five-year plans allotted only 20 percent of public-development funds for agriculture, but the government is now putting much more emphasis on that sector. In 1972 many Indian states passed legislation restricting family ownership of land. However, previous state laws were widely circumvented by the use of "dummy" holders—like the method of speculators in our own country who decades ago acquired huge tracts of public land.

As land reform illustrates, few of the changes needed in India have to do primarily with economic theory. Education is another example. Reporter Sydney H. Schanberg writes:

Standards are low in universities to accomodate the growing number of degree seekers, most of them from the middle class. The degree has become merely a status symbol, something to help in arranging an affluent marriage, not a sign of educational achievement.

Among Indian students, unlike many of their counterparts in the West, little trace of political or social idealism can be found. There is also little idealism among the members of the comfortable upper middle class, not to mention the rich. Largely an urban and Westernized class, they are dedicated to conspicuous consumption.

These examples suggest that a swing toward more free enterprise or toward more socialism would do little by itself to change attitudes that now reinforce India's poverty. But the example of a mixture of economic theories which India has followed probably will continue to be the course followed by most developing countries—also with a mixture of results.

PEOPLE | Like most discussions of development, my brief sketches fail to convey a sense of warmth for people. We can speak of "the problem" of hunger or "the problem" of poverty and in this way impersonalize them. That locution may allow us subtly, unconsciously to nourish the assumption that to be hungry or poor is to be somehow less human, with less claim to life. For this reason I find refreshing Pope Paul's reference to the poor as "guests of the banquet of life"—even if the portions served them are meager. They, too, establish bonds of love and friendship. They celebrate, as we do, the great and the small things of life. They, no less than we, attach high value to the traditions they received from their parents and pass on to their children. If their hopes are greatly circumscribed by unrelenting hardships, they hope nonetheless. Dignity, pride, pain, fear, joy—these feelings are common to all mankind.

There is likewise a personal, local dimension missing from the examples that I mention. A host of small, undramatic efforts say more about real human development than elaborate national programs. I think, for instance, of Carroll Behrhorst, a physician from Winfield, Kansas, who 23 years ago left a lucrative private practice and moved with his family to Chimaltenango, Guatemala. Starting with nothing more than a suitcase full of equipment and limited church support, he began work among poverty-stricken Cakchiquel Indians in the Chimaltenango area. Dr. Behrhorst's small clinic and hospital now serve tens of thousands of Indians each year—you can see them line up by the dozens at dawn. The clinic and the hospital are not exciting to look at, but what takes place there is exciting.

What makes this more than a standard success story is that Behrhorst early decided that medical aid alone would only increase poverty and malnutrition. With 90 percent of the children in the area malnourished, he felt he was plowing the sea. So he began, through assistants, to teach simple, scientific methods of farming, including livestock, poultry, and egg production. Behrhorst has reached out to Indians in dozens of surrounding villages by attracting from the villages young men handpicked for their leadership ability. He trains them to diagnose and treat common diseases, instruct in birth control, teach reading, and show Indian peasants modern farming methods. The position of "village worker" rapidly became a respected one, to which many young Indians now aspire, for the village worker often becomes the acknowledged village leader.

New and old village workers are constantly in training at Chimaltenango and continue to extend the network of healing and community improvement. Assistants now operate an experimental farm, and as money becomes available, the clinic buys land from large estates and sells small parcels at cost to the Indians on interest-free credit. By late 1972 not one person had defaulted on land payments, probably because the buyers can qualify for these small parcels only by agreeing to adopt scientific methods of farming. That virtually guarantees them enough production to make their payments.

Behrhorst reflects a deep respect for the Indians and their culture, and his program allows them to develop their own leadership and initiative with pride. In this way development takes place without supplanting the Indian culture with a foreign one.

As the Behrhorst program illustrates on a small scale, development usually takes place when local initiative is combined with improved opportunities, and improved opportunities are often made possible through outside assistance. Unlike our North Atlantic predecessors, who had unique advantages to seize, underdeveloped countries now have to climb out of poverty while they are being sucked more deeply into it. Soaring populations and heavy urban migration gathered momentum long before revolutions in agriculture and industry could slow the process. Today's hungry people are compelled to make their way up at a time when circumstances conspire to pull them down. But they also have some access to a fund of knowledge in science and society. Can they seize this effectively enough to make their ascent?

11

Food or Clean Air ?

As the need for development grows more urgent, poor countries face an additional handicap: the cost of pollution control. The campaign to save our environment mounts pressure against those countries to pay an extra price, as they industrialize, for not duplicating the bad habits of the West.

In reality *two* environmental campaigns are going on. One centers primarily on protecting nature and its ecosystems. The second concerns itself with social ecosystems that produce hunger, disease, and crowded hovels. By logic these two indispensable campaigns deserve to unite and strengthen each other. They could instead collide.

The first campaign is being waged by those who are not so poor. One must surmise from their rhetoric that some of them are more indignant about smog than about slums, more worried about the mistreatment of animals and lakes than about mistreated people. The effect of this may be to pit the rights of nature against human rights. A higher passion for nature is not surprising, because most U.S. citizens suffer from its abuse. Fewer of us are shorn of basics like food, shelter, medical care, work, income, and mobility.

In contrast, the second environmental struggle is prompted (if not always led) by those whose lives are battered by lack of these things. They have always struggled against nearly impossible odds, and now a new hurdle is being placed in their way. Another fee is being exacted. Rich people are upping the ante on them again. The poor of the world would probably like to breathe better air and keep their waterways pure, if they had decent jobs and enough to eat. But pollution-free hunger does not appeal to them.

CONFLICT IN THE UNITED STATES

South Carolina's Beaufort County illustrated this clash when conservationists and poor people waged what *Newsweek* called "a prototypical battle in the new age of ecology." Beaufort County achieved a certain notoriety in 1968 as one of the hunger spots of the nation. Senators and journalists toured the area to see widespread malnutrition, worm infestation, and even people with pellagra, rickets, and scurvy. The county has small clam and shrimp industries, luxury real estate developers on Hilton Head Island, and it has Port Royal Estuary, one of the few clean estuaries on the East Coast.

Late in 1969 state and local officials announced plans for a huge petrochemical industrial complex overlooking Port Royal Sound. The area polarized at once. Fishermen and real estate developers organized an impressive conservationist drive, contending that their businesses would be badly damaged and the estuary polluted. In all probability they were right. However, most of the black community fought for the plant, because new jobs, higher wages, and technical training had been promised. Local officials and anti-poverty forces geared up for an anticipated economic boom; but because of increasing bad publicity the chemical firm quietly withdrew its bid. Local environmentalists belatedly countered with a plan of their own to develop fishing, farming, and wood products in the county, with small industry located inland.

Beaufort County's experience indicates how high the stakes are, and how difficult it will be for environmentalists to shake off the suspicion that they want to keep their own surroundings tidy at the expense of the poor. The absence of poor people from "Earth Day" gatherings has told the same story. Another indication was the June, 1970, First National Congress on Optimum Population and Environment in Chicago, where black delegates staged a walkout. The unhappy delegates were not militant blacks, but members of groups such as Planned Parenthood and the National Urban League, who felt that the call for involuntary population controls would fall unequally upon their people. Before withdrawing the group stated:

It is irresponsible to use hypothetical future generations as means to escape the consequences of our failure to reorient the present-day priorities which are inconsistent with and detrimental to the interests and needs of nonwhite people.

The same year sociologist Philip Hauser warned the Population Association of America that "environmental pollution and the population explosion may be used as a smoke screen to obscure other problems which should have higher priority, including the problems of the slums, racism and 'the urban crisis' in general." President Nixon used this smoke screen in his 1970 State of the Union address. He not only singled out environmental needs as "the great question of the '70s," but added that "hard decisions" on priorities would mean refusing to spend on "programs which would benefit some of the people when their net effect would result in price increases for all the people." His words were widely understood to mean that cleaning up the environment of poverty is inflationary and must therefore give way to clean air and clean water. The Administration's attempt to slow down inflation with policies that increased unemployment was wholly consistent with this interpretation.

"The rich pollute and the poor pay," a priest told me recently. His statement contained more than a grain of truth. It is not the children of Harlem throwing beer cans into the Hudson River who make it unfit for people or fish, but the industries and municipalities upstream. The well-to-do, as high-volume consumers, make more than their share of demands on natural resources both in terms of acquisition and in terms of pollution from the manufacture of what they use. But the nonrich are expected to pay for it in more ways than one. The steel workers of Granite City, 12 miles from my home, have to go on vacation to breathe fresh air, while the top steel executives live in plush Missouri suburbs far away from the belching smokestacks. The workers and their families also pay in terms of cleaning bills, medical expenses, and impaired health. Similarly slum dwellers of most cities know that trash collection is scheduled to let garbage pile up in their streets, but not in the streets of better-heeled neighborhoods.

Now that industry faces the necessity of adopting expensive pollution-control techniques, who will pay for them? Experience indicates that U.S. citizens with low to moderate incomes will probably foot most of the bill through higher prices (the primary route) and higher taxes (to the extent that the government subsidizes environmental clean-ups). Another approach would be to cut back corporate profits, a method that stockholders and executives resist, using the plausible argument that it would curtail expansion and cost jobs. Without price increases, the cost of cleaner air and water and less noise are enough to drive many enterprises into bankruptcy.

In the end we will pay for pollution either through additional costs on the products or services we buy, or through additional medical expenses and shortened lives. The pasteurization of milk, for example, adds a fraction of a cent to each quart of milk purchased, and consumers willingly pick up the tab. Unfortunately, the cost of most antipollution measures is not so inexpensively absorbed. The only way of preventing an inordinate share of this burden from falling on people with low and moderate incomes would be through major tax reforms designed to bring about a more even distribution of income. Otherwise the wealthy will be only marginally burdened, and on the opposite end of the pole, poor people will go on expecting the fight for our natural surroundings to divert attention from *their* environment.

A DILEMMA FOR POOR COUNTRIES | If conflict between nature-environmentalists and poverty-environmentalists is noticeable in the United States, it should surprise no one to see the same conflict build up with greater intensity on a worldwide scale, and with far greater stakes for the underdeveloped countries. The stakes are high, first of all, for them to keep nature in shape. A report by former UN Secretary-General U Thant, which prompted the United Nations to convene a world Conference on the Human Environment in Stockholm in 1972, itemized the horrors of failure, such as an estimated 1.25 billion acres of productive land lost through erosion or salt poisoning. But the stakes are also high in the cost of repairing or preventing damages. Consequently many poor nations feel saddled with the dilemma of having to choose between an immediate need for food and a long-range need for a well-preserved environment—with pressure on them from the rich nations to prefer the latter. Earlier I noted that a major deficiency of U.S. politics is that decisions are made on a short-range basis rather than with the longer view in mind. If that is true of the United States, we can understand that those making political decisions in nations with much less stability are even more prone toward choices which help today, especially when the immediate stakes are so high.

A UN study on *Natural Resources of Developing Countries* advises poor countries to allocate more funds for protecting their natural resources as they pursue development projects, and it warns them not to depend on foreign aid. The report recommends a set of steps, all involving scientific skills, for carrying out the central recommendation; and it urges that this be done by the countries themselves as rapidly as their citizens can be trained to do it. This plan, in fact, makes thoroughly good sense. But if the underdeveloped countries have to carry this additional weight by themselves, when they are already struggling against hunger, they may understandably conclude that "protecting resources" is another name for staying hungry.

In 1971 Norman E. Borlaug, a key figure in the green revolution, criticized "irresponsible environmentalists" who insist that DDT and related pesticides be banned from further use. The danger of DDT is widely known. It does not readily decompose, so its components are not recycled harmlessly into the earth. Instead it finds its way into the food chain and ultimately into human bodies in increasing (though as yet very minute) quantities. Borlaug asserted that this danger has been exaggerated and that a ban on DDT would mean increased hunger and starvation in the underdeveloped countries. The Food and Agriculture Organization also considers DDT and similar pesticides vital for food production in many countries and says that "until cheap, safe and efficient substitute pesticides are produced and made easily available, there is no alternative to the judicious use of DDT, especially in the developing world, to increase agricultural productivity to feed the growing number of people on our planet."

Are the environmentalists right in sounding an alarm on DDT? They probably are. While the extent of danger is subject to widely different interpretations, it would be foolish for us to take chances. DDT cannot be recalled like cars with faulty brakes. It enters the soil and water to stay—or to make its way into the food chain.

Are Borlaug and FAO right in arguing that such pesticides are vital to food production in the underdeveloped countries? Until effective alternatives appear, they are. What we have, then, is an impasse between urgent concerns that clash head on: one an immediate necessity, the other a long-range danger. If the past is any indication, immediate necessity will not be pushed aside. People who lack food will gladly take risks on DDT.

The above example is not an isolated one. In June, 1970, the

United Auto Workers sponsored a symposium in preparation for the 1972 UN conference at Stockholm. According to a report in *The New York Times,* the symposium turned into a debate between youthful environmental enthusiasts and representatives of underdeveloped countries. "They say in Seoul, Korea, the smog is a mark of progress. It shows you're making it in American terms," complained a young Yale graduate. He had more to complain about. A director of natural resources in Venezuela said, "The legacy we can give the future of great masses in poverty is worse than the legacy of an untouched environment." According to an ambassador from Ceylon, "Two-thirds of mankind, who live in the developing regions of the world, do not share the same concern about their environment . . . as the other one-third who live in the more affluent regions." He said that pure air, fresh waters, and beauty would not be acceptable substitutes for economic progress. The delegate from Trinidad agreed. "I keep telling my colleagues that industrial pollution is not our problem, we would like to have more of it. . . ."

The question of industrial pollution is the touchiest of all, because poor nations are clearly being asked to pay costs that the rich nations did not bother paying while they became rich. At Stockholm, after bitter debate on whether or not underdeveloped countries should receive some compensation for additional costs of environmental controls, the industrialized nations, led by the United States, voted no. The cost of controlling pollution amounts to a sizable new industrial tax. With underdeveloped countries severely pressed to industrialize faster, they can hardly be blamed for resisting a cost that seems certain to make industrial expansion more difficult. Of course, those countries must take care of their environment or incur debts for its neglect. At the same time they are under strong pressure to postpone payment—like we did—and concentrate now on economic development. That type of borrowing involves serious and uncertain risks for the world, but a "pay now, eat later" policy does not strike them as entirely fair.

Underdeveloped countries may have little choice, however, because international standards are on the way. The World Bank, the UN Development Program, and various aid agencies are moving in the direction of seeking compliance, and rightly so. Trade policies will soon have to take into account the extent to which exporting countries, or particular industries, have complied with environmental standards. Otherwise countries with the lowest standards, or none at all, will have an unfair advantage in competing for markets. (We face this same problem of unfair competitive advantage between states, because some vigorously enforce strict standards and others have minimal standards, with less than minimal enforcement.)

Poor nations may be forced to resort to labor-intensive technologies, which tend to be less polluting—mules pollute less than tractors, for example, both in their production and in their use. In some cases that could produce unexpected advantages, since labor-intensive technologies help to absorb the unemployed. Even so, underdeveloped countries have to be respected when they detect a fundamental, and conceivably ruinous, liability in this new "industrial tax."

THE QUESTION OF ECONOMIC GROWTH

In 1972 the nature-poverty conflict erupted over the question of limiting economic growth. The constellation of environmental problems—more people, diminishing resources, multiplying demand for them, increasing pollution—suggested to some an imperative which flies in the face of our Western impulses: restrain growth. In a document called *Blueprint for Survival,* thirty-three British scientists detailed a proposal for "a stable society"—that is, a society without economic or numerical growth. They maintained that the earth's life-support system will be disrupted "within the lifetime of our children" if present trends of consumption and growth continue.

Two months later a group of international scientists published conclusions under the title *The Limits to Growth.* Using global data, they projected by a computerized "systems analysis" the distant consequences of continued growth. The starting assumptions fed into the computer varied, but were pessimistic on such things as the discovery and development of new resources, and the possibility of greatly reducing pollution—assumptions which rigged the outcome. ("Garbage in, garbage out," complained one critic.) Each model led ultimately to sudden collapse of growth either because of food or raw material shortages, or because of pollution. These scientists concluded that the only way to avoid an abrupt collapse would be to plan ahead for absolute limits on population, pollution, and production. That, they contended, means gradually halting economic growth.

Either a no-growth or a slow-growth situation would create an enormous dilemma for the United States alone—but nothing at all like the crisis it would present to underdeveloped countries. If there is to be a reduced rate of growth, for example, how is that growth to occur? Would the rich nations limit their own consumption of raw materials so that the poor nations could process a larger share? Or would we lock the poor nations into starvation? That prospect is by no means remote, since even most hopeful estimates concede that the earth's present population will soon be several times larger than at present. If the rich nations *now* gobble up a lopsided share of new economic growth, then under conditions of *reduced* economic growth poor nations could look forward to getting even smaller portions for their swelling populations. Clearly, to propose a leveling off of growth raises the question of where that growth is to be concentrated. And that, in turn, pushes distribution of wealth to the forefront as an urgent issue.

As I write this, the thesis that a nongrowing society offers the only alternative to ecological disaster has been adopted by relatively few scientists. Obviously we are short of absolute clarity on this matter. Global ecology is an infant science and its data still fragmentary. (We have probably spent more on space exploration than on this type of earth exploration.) The world's natural resources are not infinite. We hope to discover or learn to make use of additional raw materials, perhaps at an expanding rate, so that their availability will also increase—although estimating the extent to which this might be so necessarily pushes us into guess-work, as clashing scientific opinions indicate.

Meanwhile, as a nonscientist, I can only conclude that we have to move quickly in the direction of *more discriminately planned growth* in order to secure harmony with nature *and* justice for people. Such an approach postpones the question of the limits to growth, but it is the only effective way we have of working out an answer to that question. Meanwhile the assessment of Paul G. Hoffman, former head of the UN Development Program, applies, that "increased productivity is necessary for providing both the financial and the technical resources to undo the environmental damage that has already been done."

The heart of the matter, then, concerns not the quantity but the quality of growth. Concentrating on the quality of growth may or may not slow the rate of growth. According to environmentalist Barry Commoner, "What happens to the environment depends on *how* the growth is achieved." By itself, halting economic growth could still be part of a formula for continuing down the path of environmental disaster. As Commoner points out in *The Closing Circle,* the dramatic increase in U.S. environmental pollution since 1946 has occurred not primarily because of population growth or increased production, but because of new, pollution-intensive tech-nologies which place unprecedented burdens on the life systems of nature. It is above all these technologies (for example, those involved in the production of synthetics such as plastics, fabrics, and pesticides) that have to be dealt with if we are going to make peace with our environment.

North Americans have lived with the illusion that in exploiting nature, technologies are free. In reality they incur a huge public debt. They may produce more, but they also spoil vital parts of nature. A fairly small percentage of our population has reaped the financial benefits of this subsidy, but the entire public is now saddled with the expense of cleaning up. Undoing the damage and

gradually establishing methods of production that work in balance
with nature will require, in Commoner's estimation, more than
$40 billion a year for an entire generation—a cost, of course, that
must be measured against the cost of not moving decisively on this
problem.

If Commoner's estimate is correct, then major economic adjustments will be necessary, particularly in order to assure ordinary
citizens a chance to work and a fairer portion of the nation's
wealth. For example, he cites evidence that the intensive use of
chemical fertilizer causes unacceptable damage to our rivers and
lakes. This problem could be alleviated, he maintains, if instead of
using heavy concentrations of chemical fertilizers, we quit dumping municipal sewage into our waterways and recycled that waste
back to the farms. Some successful experimentation on this is
taking place in Michigan and Illinois. Right now it is still expensive, and some believe that it would cut back the yield per acre; if
so, it could bring economic ruin to many farmers, unless adjustments were made. If Commoner's analysis became widely established, arrangements would have to be worked out to insure the
survival of farmers through some form of income guarantees.

On the surface that kind of policy appears to subsidize the
farmer. The present technology pays its own way, we are apt to
conclude, while the proposed alternative would mean putting the
family farmer on the public dole. In reality the exact reverse is
true. To the extent that farm technology, like any technology,
causes unacceptable damage to nature, it feeds on a public subsidy,
even though that subsidy has never been written into the national
budget. Methods of soil fertilization that fall within Commoner's
acceptable limits might be less efficient in terms of production
units per acre; but such farming would pay its own way, if you
grant that part of the cost of food production is assuring the
farmer a fair return for his work.

A similar type of economic protection would have to be worked
out for those engaged—both labor and management—in the auto-
motive industry, or in any industry in which unemployment might

follow the correction of technology. It is essential for countries like our own to have alternatives ready for people thrown out of work in the affected industries. That means expanded unemployment compensation, job training programs, and guaranteed employment.

If gearing U.S. production technologies to the environment involves an assurance of a fair distribution of wealth (to the farmer, for example), this applies all the more on an international level. Just as the failure to make adjustments in the United States would probably result in economic and social disintegration here, so failure to do so on a global scale could bring about worldwide economic and social disintegration. Only international cooperation can save many of the poor nations from setbacks, as rich nations set out to make amends with nature and help establish international standards.

Because the needs of the environment move us to face the possibility of restrained growth, enormous imbalances between rich and poor nations (and to a lesser extent between lower and higher income people in the United States) push the question of economic justice to the forefront. That will not be resolved without conflict—nonviolent conflict, I hope, but intense conflict, surely.

At the same time, within this emerging conflict is the potential for a new birth of understanding. A better world view could result, because the logic of the environment, as well as the logic of human justice, calls us to deal not with separated parts, but with the whole. Perhaps that hope is an incipient fruit of the Stockholm meeting.

At Stockholm the rich nations repeatedly ducked the toughest questions. They said they do not want to help the poor nations handle the burden of meeting high environmental standards. They comprised a minority of 15 voting against a proposal by India that an international fund be established to provide countries with "seed money" for the housing environment of the poor. The United States even cast a lone vote (out of 58 nations) against a committee's recommendation that the possibility of substituting

natural materials for synthetics be investigated. Stockholm produced monumental achievements for which the world can be grateful; but its achievements are congenial to the present hierarchy of
wealth. Important as it is for monitoring our global environment,
an Earthwatch does not tinker with questions of international
justice.

Still, the Stockholm gathering offers hope—not because the
conflict between those who stressed poverty and those who stressed
nature was resolved, or even adequately faced, but because it was
dramatized. Thanks to the underdeveloped countries, Stockholm
did force this conflict to surface. It gave a standing ovation to
Prime Minister Indira Gandhi of India, who said, "How can we
speak to those who live in villages and in slums about keeping the
oceans, the rivers and the air clean, when their own lives are
contaminated at the source?" Delegates changed the Declaration of
the Human Environment to include more nearly this point of view.
In the preconference words of Barry Commoner, who attended
Stockholm as an observer: "What is just beginning to become
apparent is that the debt [to nature] cannot be paid in recycled
beer cans or in the penance of walking to work; it will need to be
paid in the ancient coins of social justice—within nations and
among them."

If we are to deal with global problems in a comprehensive
rather than fragmentary manner, then the nature-environment and
the poverty-environment movements will each have to adopt the
cause of the other as part of its own. After all, poor people *do*
have much at stake in the care of the earth. Steelworkers in Granite
City would benefit more from depolluted skies than would their
company managers, who already live where the air is comparatively clean. If lands and waters are spoiled for human use, and if
DDT works its way up the food chain in more lethal quantities,
people in underdeveloped countries, too, will suffer the consequences of such folly.

Conversely, the nonpoor have much at stake in the care of
people. A world full of poverty and hunger cannot remain an

acceptable human habitat. It certainly would not be a world in which people concentrated on the ecosystems. But for the nature-environment and poverty-environment movements to join in a common undertaking, the main burden will have to fall on the nature-environment forces to humanize their outlook and campaign for the right of people to live above squalor. Nature-environment advocates are the ones who have the luxury to adopt the poverty-environment cause, rather than vice versa, for they can do so without the distraction of putting hungry children to sleep.

Failing that, affluent people from the rich nations will certainly turn environmentalism into a self-serving and probably self-defeating enterprise. If the interdependence of life includes first and foremost the interdependence of people, then true environmentalism embraces world development. That is the kind of movement on which both rich and poor nations could unite.

Part III

U.S. POLICY

12

The Rediscovery of America

It is time for us to face an ugly truth: The United States is not seriously trying to help the human race overcome hunger and poverty. We have no vision for joining with poor countries to arrange a more livable world. Instead we let them slip toward a situation in which unmanageable conditions increasingly threaten.

This near collapse of concern has been accompanied for two decades by the enlargement of U.S. military power. *But the strength of the nation lies more in its ideals, and in the practice of those ideals, than in the flexing of national muscles.* Put another way, power is nothing new. The world has seen power as long as nations have existed, sometimes trembling before it, sometimes submitting to it, but never loving it. Others have often loved the United States, but seldom for its power. Rather what captured the admiration of people throughout the world was the fact that, for all its faults and contradictions, this country wrested its independence from England and started a new experiment in freedom. In setting out the nation's course, its founding leaders declared that "all men are created equal," and they determined to shape the nation's destiny along democratic lines.

This may sound like useless sentiment to youth, impatient with glaring inconsistencies between the nation's stated ideals and its practices. But it is a mistake to brush history aside, because we need to draw on the roots of our past for guidance. Without doing so we can achieve neither self-understanding nor a sense of national purpose sufficient to give us the capacity for improvement.

To invoke national ideals is not to deny fundamental departures. Freedom for the colonists and pioneers also meant freedom to seize land from the Indians, and to make slaves or second-class citizens of black people. Such blots on our past obviously do us no credit. But at least it is possible to recognize them as contradictions to be resolved, because they patently failed to harmonize with the principles upon which the nation was established.

Those who settled in our land came with no unified set of principles. They were dissenters, religious refugees, acquisitive people, adventurers, people fleeing depression and famine, fugitives from justice, rich and poor people, good and bad. They represented a host of national and cultural backgrounds. But to an extent without precedent they made this a country where freedom and democracy were celebrated, if not always honored in practice. The United States of America was more than an emerging nation. It became a *movement,* rooted in the equality of man, and embodying the hope of "liberty and justice for all."

The lessons of the nation's past, however, tell us that liberty and justice cannot be secured for ourselves and kept from others without turning sour. Because we have cherished liberty for others, this country has sacrificed enormously (if not always wisely) in lives and material resources. We have not cherished justice as much. But justice and equality are no less a part of the nation's ideals, and we build on them by exercising them in our relationship with others. When we are rich and others are impoverished beyond description, justice calls for ending this imbalance. To a man with hungry children, justice can only be understood if it comes in the form of bread.

We do well to remember the strength of these ideals, for without them we are like Samson shorn of his hair. Some years ago, as a young newspaper editor attending a meeting of the Illinois Press Association, I had occasion to reply briefly to an address by Orval Faubus, then Governor of Arkansas, who in the guise of patriotism defended his use of National Guardsmen to defy the U.S. Supreme Court regarding segregation at Central High School in Little Rock. I had been studying conditions in North Africa and the Middle East when the Little Rock episode broke out, and I told the assembly that everywhere I traveled newspaper headlines proclaimed and people commented emotionally about the travesty of justice in the United States. The governor's defiance had clearly given our country a shameful image, and communists were making hay of it. The governor's reply—which to my surprise secured a fair round of applause from newspaper editors—was simply, "We don't give a damn what the communists think." It sounded tough. But Mr. Faubus's answer showed, among other things, a remarkable ignorance of international realities and the nature of U.S. influence abroad. Internally and internationally, the strength of our nation lies in its ideals.

Unfortunately, *we have relied too much on raw power.* Contrary to some critics on the left, the shift toward power was not cynical. In part the circumstances of history thrust it upon us, and in part it grew out of a misunderstanding. Until the end of World War II, much of the underdeveloped world knew the United States as the champion of self-determination. To many we were heroes. We stood for an end to colonialism and for freedom to the colonies. After World War II a new factor emerged—the extension of communist domination over Eastern Europe and success of the communists in China. The communist takeover in Eastern Europe and the threat of similar developments in Greece and Turkey were viewed with alarm as a new form of colonialism, and as such prompted a vigorous military buildup under our sponsorship, beginning with the NATO countries of Western Europe.

This militant anticommunist stance took place as the *continuation* of our opposition to colonialism; however, it locked us into an oversimplified interpretation. The communist revolution in China, for example, did not turn out to be part of a Soviet conquest, but a nationalist uprising with a hard-line Marxist ideology. In fact the USSR reacted to "losing" China far more intemperately than we did. (We vilified our China experts, Stalin executed his.) The same oversimplified interpretation, however well motivated, prevented us from understanding Vietnam and led to the tragedy of military intervention there.

Vietnam can only be understood against a century-long background of colonialism. Like most of today's underdeveloped world, Indochina was gobbled up by a European power. France, anxious for the grandeur of empire, forced its way into Vietnam in 1857 and fought for decades to control Indochina. Armed resistance never disappeared in that colony. The Vietnamese, unified somewhat by language and by a long history of opposition to Chinese invaders, drew strength from a nationalism already well established.

Under France, the gap between rich and poor widened. In *Asian Drama* Gunnar Myrdal reports:

> The Vietnamese were generally excluded from the modern sectors of their economy as well as from higher posts in the government. Banking, mining, large-scale manufacturing industry, and rubber production were jealously guarded French preserves. . . . In addition, French settlers, usually of peasant stock and with a background of service in the lower ranks of the French army, acquired large amounts of land. . . .

Myrdal also found that "Frenchmen of lower-class origin" occupied positions in government and business for which, by contrast, the British in India trained Indians. This practice of the French excluded the Indochinese still more.

France forcibly repressed movements toward eventual self-rule so that moderate nationalism had no chance to emerge in Vietnam. They prohibited political parties and trade unions. The consequence, writes Myrdal, "was to leave the underground Communist Party in the forefront of the Vietnamese struggle for independence." The French, who in effect recruited for the communist movement, could claim that in fighting Vietnamese nationalists they were fighting communism.

President Roosevelt wanted France out and Indochina independent, much to De Gaulle's displeasure. In 1944 Roosevelt wrote to Cordell Hull:

France has had the country—thirty million inhabitants—for nearly one hundred years, and the people are worse off than they were at the beginning. . . . France has milked it for one hundred years. The people of Indochina are entitled to something better than that.

In 1947 Secretary of State George C. Marshall advised France to make peace with Ho Chi Minh on generous terms, and warned that continuing the war or attempting to set up a puppet government might play into the hands of communists throughout Asia by putting democracies in a bad light. Despite this warning, the United States began to support French colonialism once more, paying for 80 percent of France's war by 1954 and then finally— as far as the Vietnamese understood it—replacing France as the colonial power.

One reason we misread Vietnam, ironically, is that our record of colonial rule (in the Philippines, for example) was benevolent compared with that of the French. As a result we failed to understand the intense feeling of the Vietnamese against foreign intervention, or why our intervention, so well intended—we sought neither empire nor profit—should meet with such hostility. So instead of encountering a situation analogous to Korea in Vietnam, we reaped the consequences of a century of French misrule and were forced to defend corrupt regimes that had little popular support.

Vietnam illustrates, rather than contradicts, the fact that our military commitments abroad and the enormous sacrifices these entailed were motivated primarily by a desire to prevent another colonial power (or powers) from gobbling up helpless countries. In the process, however, the United States has placed itself in the unpopular role of world policeman, accused of practicing the colonialism we sought to prevent. Because that role involves a shift away from influence by example and toward influence by power, it obscures our ideals, and in the long run undermines our purposes.

The use of the struggle against communism as our primary tool for measuring situations abroad is a mistake for several reasons. It is a negative approach; we define ourselves by what we are *against* rather than by what we are *for*. That distorts. We cannot base a convincing program on our ideals and project it to the world by stressing what we oppose.

The approach is also based on fear. It shows an excessive awe of communism and too little confidence in democracy. We must be realistic and recognize the threat which the communist mixture of totalitarianism and idealism still represents. We cannot ignore what happened to Hungary and Czechoslovakia. But the facts do not support a position of abject fear, of mental paralysis. Do not setbacks to communism during the 1960s in the underdeveloped world, because of domestic reactions against it—Indonesia and Ghana, for examples—dispel the myth of communist invincibility? Do not fundamental splits between communist countries likewise lay to rest the phantom of a completely monolithic international movement against us?

In addition this negative approach is wrong because the problems that communism depends upon for winning converts—poverty, inequality, repression—are successfully attacked not with guns, but with social reforms and basic economic gains.

Our preoccupation with anticommunism has also moved us toward the support of too many totalitarian regimes, a stance that clearly violates the ideals we want to promote. To talk about ideals is not enough. Echoing his predecessor on Vietnam, President Nixon assured the nation that we were "only fighting for the right

of people far away to choose the kind of government they want."
But the runner-up to President Thieu in South Vietnam's 1967
election was in prison, and Thieu's one-man contest in 1971 con-
firmed widespread evidence of democracy's absence in Saigon.
Further, while Nixon spoke, the United States was shipping arms
to the Pakistani government, which was engaged in savage repression of the people of East Pakistan, who *had* expressed their will
in contested elections. We cannot expect developing nations to be
immediate, mature, full-blown democracies, obviously, but our
policies should encourage a free expression by the people in any
country.

Greece, the birthplace of democracy, is another case in point. In
1967 a group of army colonels seized power, suspended constitutional rights during a period of acknowledged national chaos, and
shut down parliament. A thousand-page report by the 15 nations
of the Council of Europe, which subsequently expelled Greece
from the Council, documented cases of brutality and torture.
Washington, however, ignored the Council and in 1970 resumed
full shipment of heavy arms to Greece. Business, as well as the
government, was implicated when in April of 1971 Secretary of
Commerce Maurice H. Stans spoke in Athens before high-ranking
government officials:

> We in the United States government, particularly in American busi-
> ness, greatly appreciate Greece's attitude toward American investment,
> and we appreciate the welcome that is given here to American com-
> panies and the sense of security that the government of Greece is im-
> parting to them.

Too much reliance on power, coupled with fear of communism,
has even led us to take part in misguided military interventions.
Vietnam is not the only example. Nineteen sixty-one found us
deeply involved in the Bay of Pigs fiasco in Cuba. In 1965 the
U.S. Marines invaded the Dominican Republic to dismantle a
reformist revolution that had seized power. Regarding that intru-
sion, Senator William J. Fulbright has written:

The central fact about the intervention of the United States in the Dominican Republic was that we had closed our minds to the causes and to the essential legitimacy of revolution in a country in which democratic procedures had failed. The involvement of an undetermined number of communists in the Dominican Revolution was judged to discredit the entire reformist movement, like poison in a well, and rather than use our considerable resources to compete with the communists for influence with the democratic forces who actively solicited our support, we intervened militarily on the side of a corrupt and reactionary military oligarchy. We thus lent credence to the idea that the United States is the enemy of social revolution, and therefore the enemy of social justice, in Latin America.

Opposition to communism as a guiding star in foreign affairs leads us to postures that are ludicrous when measured by traditional U.S. ideals. Allende's Chile, because it elected a Marxist administration through the democratic process, was unworthy of a common U.S. naval courtesy, but the White House received General Medici, head of Brazil's hard-line military dictatorship, as an honored guest. And after the Pakistani army had for eight months committed crimes enough to force ten million Bengalis to flee into India, our President publicly commended that country's ruler, General Yahya Khan, for his efforts "to reduce tensions in the subcontinent." I do not mean by this to single out the Nixon Administration for criticism. The leadership of both political parties has, with good intentions, erred in its eagerness to bolster governments that set themselves against communism, but in doing so it has not led the United States to pay "a decent respect to the opinions of mankind" which the Declaration of Independence commends to us. Because public opinion also represents great power, this has weakened our influence in the world community.

Most important of all, our preoccupation with communism has led to "benign neglect" of hunger and poverty abroad, a neglect which fails monumentally to keep faith with the nation's ideals. Adrift from these moorings, we have lacked the capacity to initiate a global development program of the magnitude and quality that would once again evoke deep admiration for the United States. Anchored in our ideals, we could easily lead a massive, worldwide effort to reduce hunger and poverty. Providing such leadership entails fundamental changes in our approach toward (1) trade; (2) investment; (3) economic assistance; and (4) the military.

13

Trade, Free and Fair

As most of us learned from our childhood friends, trade is an exchange freely agreed upon between parties so that each secures a benefit. That idea remains the working model for nations as well, but in practice the benefits tend to favor rich countries and tag poor ones as losers. This troublesome fact suggests that in its own policy the United States adopt several overdue reforms in order to move toward the goal of equitable trade. Otherwise, for the sake of a few short-range advantages this nation will be spreading hunger and poverty abroad.

The United States should remove barriers to free trade. The resurgence of protectionism reflects a short-sighted grasp of world realities, as well as defective leadership. Protective tariffs and import quotas work a particular hardship on poor countries, which need to develop markets as they industrialize. Virtually all economists agree that these barriers need to be reduced, if not eliminated, and the trend for several decades has been in that direction. Still, barriers are maintained and occasionally enlarged. The period of the early 1970s was marked by rising protectionist fever because industries with jobs and profits at stake created a vocal, grass-roots lobby.

Trade barriers hand each of us a sizable bill. They hurt much of the world's economy, and in the long run that hinders our own. There are immediate costs, too. Tariffs and quotas on goods coming into the United States result in higher prices, along with the inflationary effects of those prices—a cost to the U.S. consumer, estimated by Malgren and Krimmins, of $10 to $15 billion a year, or from $200 to $300 per family. Trade barriers also hurt our export industries. First, by making it hard for poor countries to expand exports, trade barriers sharply curtail their ability to buy from us. Second, they insure that other countries will impose trade restrictions against us. That is a penalty of sizable consequence, because over the years our exports have greatly exceeded our imports—the U.S. trade deficit of $3 billion in 1971 was our first calendar-year deficit since 1888.

Nineteen seventy-one marked a new ball game, with other countries increasingly able to compete against us in some low-wage areas. Industries estimated that in 1971 imports would account for the following percentage of U.S. purchases of these products:

> Home radios, 90%
> Black & white TVs, 51%
> Shoes, 42%
> New cars, 16%
> Motorcycles, 96%
> Sweaters, 68%

By 1972 the U.S. trade deficit reached $6.4 billion, a deficit attributable entirely to trade with other rich nations. Although we still sold as much to the *poor* countries as we bought from them, their competitive ability is growing and would get a substantial boost if trade barriers were lifted. But protectionism provides a costly solution because in effect it subsidizes our production weaknesses and handicaps our production strengths, a policy which results in *less real national wealth*. A great majority of economists stress that in order to maintain a competitive edge, the United States needs to specialize in areas of comparative advantage, such as higher-technology products.

Economist Paul A. Samuelson, winner of the Nobel Prize, speaks for many of his colleagues when he sees the United States (1) shifting its emphasis from manufacturing to services; (2) accepting as normal an unfavorable balance of trade in consumer goods; (3) paying for this through investment earnings abroad; (4) having a more productive economy as a result; and (5) protecting U.S. workers and industries, not with trade barriers but with other guarantees.

More important than their disadvantages to us, trade barriers impose an unacceptable burden on the poor nations, as they try to expand their industries and exports associated with them. For us the issue concerns degrees of abundance; for them it concerns human survival.

I have already pointed out that agricultural protectionism makes it hard for poor countries to expand farm exports. This constitutes a major obstacle to their development, and to the reduction of hunger. By one estimate, a concession of 2 percent in agricultural self-sufficiency by the rich nations would be worth $4 billion annually in export earnings to the underdeveloped countries.

In addition the United States increases tariffs on products as they become more highly processed, protecting most of all labor-intensive industries that compete well with some of our own—an obvious discouragement to industrial development in the poor countries. Import quotas work a similar disadvantage. According to one observer:

> Our policy has been to support the industrialization of Latin American countries until it reached the point where some of its products were marketable, and then to jam on the brakes. Thus, the ideal aid recipient, from the U.S. point of view, has been a country which can accept development assistance indefinitely, without making any progress.

In one instance the United States loaned money to a Latin American country for a cotton glove manufacturing plant. After the plant was built, a North Carolina firm placed an order for 12 million pair a year. Upon advice of the U.S. Tariff Commission, however, the White House restricted the glove company to a quota of 20,000 pair, thus jamming on the brakes.

Oil import quotas present a particularly annoying example to U.S. consumers. According to President Nixon's own cabinet-level Task Force on Oil Import Control, these quotas cost consumers an extra $5 billion in 1970. It estimated that by 1980 the cost would rise to $8.4 billion, or approximately $65 billion for this decade alone. Thus a quota imposed for reasons of "national security"— unnecessarily, according to the task force—lets a handful of oil men make additional fortunes that show in higher fuel bills for each of us.

Movement toward free trade is not enough, however. The removal of barriers will not, by itself, enable poor nations to trade with us on an equal basis, because we hold too many advantages. Poor nations suffer because the price of raw materials (their main exports) tends to decline in relation to manufactured products (their main imports). Combined with quota and tariff restrictions against their manufactured goods, these worsening terms of trade act as an imposing obstacle to development. *The Christian Century* describes the squeeze this way:

> Caught between rising prices on their industrial imports and falling export prices—and effectively excluded from exporting their own industrial products—Asian, African and Latin American leaders of all ideological hues have been driven toward a Marxist cynicism about the world economy.

That kind of desperation is hard for us to feel. Nevertheless we get an inkling of it by noting the anger of our own trade officials toward Japan. John K. Jessup summarized the reason for that anger in a *Life* magazine article, "How the Japanese Got So Rich So Fast":

> . . . the Japanese treat us the way prewar Belgians or the Dutch used to treat their colonies. They buy chiefly our raw materials—lumber, cot-

ton, wheat, coal, soybeans—and sell us a wide range of high-technology, high-profit manufactured goods. If this trend continues, the U.S. trade deficit with Japan could be $4 billion by 1973.

As it turned out, we reached the $4 billion trade deficit with Japan in 1972. Apart from the particularized items, what Jessup describes is exactly the position many underdeveloped countries find themselves in *vis-à-vis* the United States—only without the resources to make up for it in other ways or the leverage to fight back.

This top-heavy arrangement could be turned around partly by working out greater stability in prices on many raw materials. More important, the United States could gradually eliminate tariffs on imports from underdeveloped countries, while still allowing those countries to protect their infant industries. Such an arrangement could hand them, on a small scale, the kind of advantage we have enjoyed up to now. Although the United States has endorsed the principle of tariff preferences, it has yet to act on that principle.

The use of price agreements and tariff preferences qualifies but does not set aside the goal of free trade. Free trade would still apply to trading equals and affect the great majority of exports and imports. By allowing underdeveloped countries temporary advantages, however, this approach makes free trade a less absolute goal than fair trade, although it would move the world toward both in an overall sense. By the same token of fairness, countries like our own need to proceed gradually in order to cushion themselves against a sudden influx of products from abroad, and to give their economies time to adjust.

Fair trade and free trade are achievable goals—if we have committed leadership. In April, 1972, the *Journal of Commerce* observed—approvingly:

The administration has stalled on its contribution to the International Development Association [the World Bank's soft loan division]. It doesn't want any special allocation of . . . special drawing rights to the LDCs [less developed countries] in excess of their normal quotas. It won't consider preferential tariffs for the time being. It doesn't want to see the LDCs ordering half or more of their trade to be routed in their own ships. And it seems in no hurry to make the monetary adjustments that could make the U.S. market more lucrative for overseas commodity exports.

In other words, just about every major proposal put forth in the interests of protecting the LDCs from further deterioration in their terms of trade is drawing a negative reaction in Washington.

The United States can do better than that.

A generous trade policy must be coupled with a thorough adjustment program at home. Labor is rightly concerned about the loss of jobs in industries that face a new competitive challenge from abroad. Business and the farm sector also have serious concerns. Businesses which suffer because of foreign imports should have low-interest, government-guaranteed loans available to them so that they can become competitive again or move into other areas of production.

The same approach applies to agriculture, as we open markets for underdeveloped countries. A U.S. farm program that encourages the family farmer and stimulates world food distribution while it encourages developing nations, is long overdue. Within this framework some of the gains the public makes in lower food prices and reduced subsidies to wealthy farm operators can be applied to a program of adjustment for those family farmers and farm workers who are adversely affected.

Some of labor's anxiety centers on the exporting of jobs by U.S. firms that transfer their capital and technology to an underdeveloped country, where an affiliate can turn out products at wages that range up to ten times lower than in the United States. But if we are to reap the benefits of rationalizing the world's production and distribution, then we must also rationalize production and distribution in the United States so that workers in adversely affected industries can turn to acceptable alternatives.

The answer is to guarantee a job to all within the United States, in the private sector in so far as possible, but with the government as the employer of last resort. The entire society then assumes the adjustment burden—and the entire society will benefit from a reduction in crime, welfare costs, and other things that plague us partly because of our high unemployment. In addition, we can do more work on long neglected needs: rebuilding cities, improving our environment, our schools, and our health services.

Aside from the trade issue, this kind of domestic program needs to be enacted anyway.

The policy of guaranteed work within the United States is important to the underdeveloped countries because its adoption would make possible greater labor support of a generous trade program. Without a policy of guaranteed employment U.S. workers will constantly fear that gains abroad may eliminate their jobs. The nation now generates internal pressure for frustrating the aspirations of hungry people around the globe.

With a policy of guaranteed employment, of assistance to the family farmer, and of low-interest loans to the company making adjustments because of trade pattern changes, all of these sectors can play key roles in supporting a policy of expanding trade opportunities for underdeveloped countries.

14

Profits Abroad

If the United States makes possible new development opportunities for poverty-ridden nations by giving them trade preferences—if both we and they are to benefit from the comparative advantages of each—then U.S. investments abroad must grow and return profits in order to at least partly offset resulting trade deficits.

Total U.S. investments abroad climbed from $32 billion in 1960 to $86 billion in 1971, when they returned $10 billion in earnings to the United States. According to President Nixon's Council of Economic Advisers, those earnings will reach $17 billion by 1975. When trade deficits are measured against these profits, the financial balance solidly favors the United States. In view of this we may ask: Is it worthy of our nation, with a national output more than double that of the entire underdeveloped world, to deny poor countries fair trade?

The answer obviously is no, and that means we must offer trade preferences. Trade preferences, however, not only justify but necessitate U.S. investment profits in other countries. The crucial need in that case is *to build investments abroad with-*

out building economic empires. The model should be that of private enterprise helping to service development for a reasonable return.

Are business ventures abroad compatible with the requirements of development in the poor nations? Not necessarily. Private enterprise thrives on the profit motive. Companies go to unfamiliar lands, where the risks and difficulties tend to be abnormal, because they expect to make a return on their investment great enough to offset possible disadvantages. This applies pressure for a "quick kill" on profits, or for excessive long-range returns, a situation that often counteracts healthy growth in those countries.

On the other hand, high profits may reflect efficiency rather than greed. Contrary to Marx, the fact that private enterprise looks for profits does not make it evil. But with few exceptions private enterprise does put money, not humanitarian objectives, up front. That impulse has to be taken candidly into account, because the profit motive harmonizes no more naturally with development needs than it does with environmental needs. Business abroad can be a public servant—or an economic monster—and U.S. policy should recognize both possibilities.

While underdeveloped areas account for only a third of U.S. investments abroad, the impact of investments there is far greater than comparable holdings in rich, industrialized nations. This applies especially to Latin America, where extreme inequalities make it all the more vulnerable. In 1970 Gunnar Myrdal estimated:

. . . directly or indirectly, through joint enterprises and other arrangements, United States corporations now control or decisively influence between 70 and 90 percent of the raw-material resources of Latin America, and probably more than half of its modern manufacturing industry, banking, commerce, and foreign trade, as well as much of its public utilities.

Another cause for alarm in Latin America is growing U.S. dominance in the communications media, which promote extravagant consumer tastes that militate against development needs.

You can appreciate the feeling of many Latins that they are being swallowed up, remembering that in the mid-1960s even Europeans began to complain bitterly that U.S. corporations were turning their countries into economic colonies. By consolidating efforts, however, Europe, with its advanced technology and strong economies, has been able to stand up well against this threat. To a much lesser extent so has Canada, even though most of its industry is U.S. owned and controlled.

Not always so the poor nations. For them the issue concerns economic control; the loss of profits and of raw materials without commensurate gains, such as export markets for manufactured goods; the bringing in of capital-intensive technology that creates few jobs and spreads few benefits; the promotion of luxury products; and the recurring practice of bribing officials in order to secure privileges—a tax-deductible business expense for U.S. firms.

Comparative advantage, they know too well, can mean *taking* advantage. Investing firms have more bargaining chips and can shop around for the best incentives. This puts enormous pressure on countries, inundated with hunger and poverty, to seek industries on any possible terms. The growing need of large multinational firms (three-fourths of which are U.S. corporations) to invest abroad in order to compete well is making the bargaining less unequal. But it will take fair trade opportunities, as well as farsighted development policies and collective determination on the part of underdeveloped nations, in order to achieve a situation in which genuine comparative advantage is the rule.

There is another reason we cannot shrug off responsibility for economic greed abroad. Because change often shakes stability and creates an atmosphere less conducive to making profits, U.S. business interests tend to discourage our government from favoring needed reforms. This influence helped to scuttle the Alliance for Progress, as investments were talked up and reforms talked down. By preferring short-term stability to boat-rocking change, U.S. enterprise abroad has also frequently encouraged this nation to back repressive governments. Hindering civil liberties in this way cultivates for U.S. business a reputation that contradicts the freedom it espouses at home.

This quest by business for stability unfortunately dovetails with the State Department's tendency to give stability abroad a higher rating than democracy, when Cold War advantages are perceived. An overriding preference for stability, combined with investment practices that tend to hinder rather than assist the poor, causes Western industrialists to play into the hands of both communist and right-wing extremists who need above all to convince people that gradualism through democracy offers no hope for improvement. Marxist cynicism is fostered and totalitarianism can present itself more plausibly as an alternative.

These considerations do not lead to the conclusion that U.S. business investments are always at loggerheads with the needs of underdeveloped countries. Rather they lead us away from the assumption that such ventures *automatically* contribute to development and require no restraints. Many of them do contribute to development; many do not. Just as British capital helped to finance industrial growth in the United States during the last century, so the capital and skills that Western firms now bring to underdeveloped countries can be invaluable, *provided they fulfill real development needs.* That is less brash, less arrogant, and perhaps even a less profitable role than the one we are accustomed to. It reflects the real world with painful, stubborn problems, not a tidy, make-believe world whose needs always coincide with our ambitions. But it is a role that can work out to the mutual advantage of both company and underdeveloped country.

The rest of the 1970s may accelerate a movement toward nationalization of foreign-owned industries, and underdeveloped countries will almost certainly insist on more favorable arrangements from foreign investors. U.S. government and business leaders do well to anticipate these trends with enlightened policies.

Chilean nationalization of the copper mines is a case in point. Chile has the world's largest reserve of copper. It is of exceptionally high grade, and it accounts for almost 80 percent of Chile's exports. According to a statement by the Chilean government in 1971:

The working of Chilean copper mines by U.S. companies constitutes in fact a truly colonial hold on our country and on the Chilean economy. Chile is prevented from taking sovereign decisions regarding all basic aspects of this industry which forms the heart of our economic life. . . . Such decisions are made in New York.

Because the U.S. companies had their own processing firms, Chile declared, they sold copper to themselves at a price well below the world market. The Chilean government contends that in copper, iron, and nitrate industries, U.S. firms made small initial investments, with further investments derived from the local operations.

Chile's figures show that from 1955 to 1970 Anaconda's investments there were 16.64 percent of its worldwide total, while its profits in Chile were 79.24 percent of that total. Kennecott showed a 13.16 percent investment in Chile for the same period, with profits from Chile of 21.37 percent of its total. The Chilean government, which stressed that it was buying the copper industry, not confiscating it, insisted that excessive profits would be taken into account in determining a fair price. Subsequently the government announced that such profits far exceeded the value of the copper mines, and by late 1972 prospects of the companies recovering more than a small fraction of their claims seemed dim. Chile's withholding compensation may be both unwise and unwarranted. In assessing this, however, we have to imagine how we would feel if Latins had owned U.S. auto and steel industries, and carted off the profits for 60 years. After all, the celebrated Boston Tea Party acted against "taxation without representation," and the wish of a country to keep its own basic industries out of foreign control is not entirely alien to that spirit.

Alternatives to repeating the imbalances of the past are being put forward. In an essay, *How to Divest in Latin America and Why*, Albert O. Hirschman suggests inducing new investments by permitting higher initial profits, but with ownership automatically reverting to nationals after a specified number of years. The suggestion includes training nationals in management and technical skills. For existing foreign-owned industries, Hirschman favors an arrangement which permits local investors—preferably white- and blue-collar workers, especially those working in companies—to buy up those industries. He proposes an Inter-American Divestment Corporation which could assist in this by acquiring ownership until local purchasers are found. An approach along this line is likely to gain favor among foreign investors as pressures against them mount. Or perhaps all types of ownership will be increasingly closed to foreigners, and U.S. firms will export by contract their management and technical skills to the underdeveloped countries.

The United States should be prepared to honor reasonable solutions, because we are not obliged to mortgage our ideals for the excesses of a few companies. It is possible for rich and poor countries to work out investment agreements that serve the development needs of each. U.S. profits on investments abroad and export earnings of underdeveloped countries could stimulate each other in a benevolent cycle of growth.

15

Foreign Aid: A Case of Intentions

If the purpose of U.S. economic assistance is to move people away from hunger and poverty by spurring development, then it falls far short of the mark. One reason for this failure is that *aid to the underdeveloped countries, never sufficient to begin with, began dropping in the 1960s.* To say that *insufficient* foreign aid is a cause of failure pays indirect tribute to the considerable accomplishments of such aid, without which the world would be in much worse condition today.

Foreign aid is a relatively new idea. A precedent of sorts began during World War II with "lend-lease," which enabled our allies to carry on the war effort. When the war ended in 1945, so did the lend-lease program. Soon it became apparent that the nations of Europe were not able to rise quickly from the ashes and rebuild themselves. Spurred by this and by fear of Soviet communism, in 1947 the United States proposed a European Recovery Program (the Marshall Plan). Including postwar relief that predated the Marshall Plan, and apart from military aid, the United States poured $23.1 billion worth of official economic assistance—plus much private assistance—into Western Europe from 1946 to 1952. By then Western Europe seemed well on the way toward a miraculous recovery. The United States also offered Marshall Plan aid to Eastern European countries, but they rejected it.

In his 1949 inaugural address, President Truman proposed "a bold new program for making the benefits of our scientific advances and industrial progress available for the improvement and growth of underdeveloped areas." Truman's "Point Four Program" (it was point four of his inaugural address) suggested that what began for Europe would now be extended to the poor nations. The Marshall Plan, the Point Four Program, and Truman's appeal to the UN for a technical assistance program were creative, visionary proposals that kept faith with U.S. ideals and rallied the best impulses of the nation.

By far the greatest concentration of our aid went to Western Europe. During the four-year period from 1949 to 1952 the United States sent more than $12 billion as outright grants (aside from loans) to Western Europe in the form of official development assistance. By comparison we gave all of Latin America $5 billion in economic grants spread over 25 years from 1946 to 1970. During the same 25-year period our economic grants to all underdeveloped countries totaled $40.5 billion, but $15.5 billion of that was concentrated in a few countries with acute security needs (Greece, Turkey, Formosa, Indochina, and South Korea), whose people comprised no more than 5 percent of the population of the poor countries. We allotted approximately $1 billion a year in economic grants to the other 95 percent of the underdeveloped world. Europe—part of the rich, industrialized world—received a much higher concentration of aid from us than did impoverished countries that collectively have a population nine times greater than Western Europe's. The contrast is made even more severe when dollar values are adjusted to offset the effect of inflation.

Why this imbalance? And why has assistance tapered off?

The imbalance developed partly because European countries had been ravaged by war, so U.S. aid came in response to a calamity in which we had also suffered. In addition most citizens of the United States trace their backgrounds to Europe, and millions of them still had close relatives there after the war. As a result, a powerful grass-roots lobby existed in virtually every congressional district across the land for promoting the Marshall Plan. Still another reason was that the results of our aid to Europe were immediate and dramatic. In contrast to the underdeveloped countries, Europe already had advanced technology, education, skills, work habits, and many of the necessary facilities. There we helped economies disrupted by the war get back on their feet. All Europeans needed was a boost so that they could put their experience to work again. The poor nations began with none of these advantages, and we spread aid to them exceedingly thin by comparison. Not surprisingly, the results disappointed the U.S. public.

Aid tapered off also because taxpayers have been led to believe that they spend much more on economic assistance than is the case. Few people realize that the United States now ranks near the bottom among rich nations in aid to poor countries, when aid is figured as a percentage of national production. By the most generous estimates the United States is providing proportionately less assistance (including official and officially-guaranteed loans) to the underdeveloped countries than Australia, Belgium, Canada, Denmark, France, Germany, the Netherlands, Norway, Sweden, and Great Britain. At its peak in 1949, our assistance to Europe reached almost 3 percent of our Gross National Product and over 11 percent of the federal budget. According to the U.S. Agency for International Development, by 1971 all forms of economic assistance combined represented not 3 percent but *three-tenths of 1 percent* of our GNP and about 1½ percent of the federal budget.

Even those figures are padded. The Nixon Administration's proposed national budget for fiscal year 1973 requests $3.3 billion for official development assistance. To unpad, deduct $629* million for principal and interest payments on previous loans; $796

* The 1971 repayment.

million for supporting assistance, mostly to Indochina, which rightfully belongs under the category of military aid; $181 million for 20 percent value lost on new grants and loans because they are tied to purchases in the United States; and $420 million (50 percent) of our Food for Peace program for various nonaid factors that I explain below. That chops the budgeted figure for development assistance down to $1.3 billion, *about one-tenth of 1 percent of our GNP,* and a cost to each citizen of less than two cents a day.

President Nixon's announced cutback in economic assistance in 1971 to help meet the U.S. balance of payments problem merely played along with a public illusion regarding the extent of our aid to poor nations. The balance of payments is not greatly affected by such assistance in any case, since about 90 percent of it is spent in the United States. In fact the U.S. Agency for International Development points out, "The relatively small proportion of AID funds spent overseas each year is more than offset by receipts of interest and repayments on past AID loans, *resulting in a net inflow* to the United States from these operations [italics mine]." While a net inflow of dollars does not detract from the fact that there is a real flowing out of U.S. resources through assistance, it does show that we get sizable compensations. According to an estimate from the Overseas Development Council, "Since we have a high rate of unemployment and large unused productive capacity, the economic cost of aid to us [in 1971] was probably near zero."

Even government shipments of food are by no means a giveaway program. As President Nixon's Task Force on International Development candidly states, "More than half the budgetary cost would be required in any event to support farm incomes in the United States." When this 50 percent savings is taken into account, a cost-benefit analysis of $16.2 billion of commodity shipments under Public Law 480 from 1955 to 1969 shows that the U.S. loss is minimal. We received payment in foreign currencies for most of the $16.2 billion. Some of this has been loaned out again (and is being repaid) for development purposes, but half of the amount, $8.1 billion, was used to pay for embassy costs and other U.S. government expenses overseas, sold in exchange for dollars or other convertible currency, or used by the Defense Department for military purposes. In short, other countries paid for most of the food, and it returned billions of dollars to the United States that would have been lost, if the food had been shipped abroad on a pure grant basis. In addition, according to the U.S. government, "Public Law 480 yields substantial balance of payments benefits to the United States." A government report estimated the balance-of-payments benefits for 1970 at $322 million.

I do not deny that P.L. 480 shipments contain a substantial element of assistance. But I stress that the economic benefit *we* receive from food shipments should also be taken into account, because in the public mind assistance constitutes a greatly exaggerated burden to taxpayers, who mount pressure for cutbacks in foreign aid.

Aid to the underdeveloped countries diminished in part because enthusiasm for a cause is hard to sustain, and people get tired of making sacrifices. Examples of waste or corruption in the use of aid—usually blown out of proportion—have caused some disaffection. The lack of gratitude and even signs of anti-Americanism in recipient nations further diminished incentive. In part this came about as a result of White House efforts to "sell" foreign aid to the public and the Congress by stressing that it served our own best interests. It did—it proved a boon to business, for example—but it also sprang from humanitarian impulses. U.S. citizens never bought the "self-interest" explanation completely. Many of them supported foreign aid because they wanted to help people. For the most part these citizens expected gratitude, and (it seemed from news reports) they got insults instead.

Along with the myth that most foreign aid is wasted has grown the belief that it benefits only the rich. It is true, of course, that assistance has not always and sufficiently reached the poor. Assistance tends to accommodate itself to, rather than challenge, the division of wealth within a receiving country. Yet on the whole aid programs *have* benefited primarily poor people. Still, the U.S. public's impression of foreign aid as help-for-the-rich has far outstripped the fact, and this has undermined public support.

More recently disenchantment has come from ardent internationalists who claim that foreign aid has become captive to the mistaken understanding of this nation's role in the world. That leads to the second major reason economic assistance has failed to spur higher levels of development: *The purpose of spurring development has been sidetracked and aid has been promoted instead for other purposes, especially as a tool for stopping communism.* The "other purposes," far from hidden, have been openly used in order to win public support and get appropriations through Congress. Quite possibly without this motivation U.S. assistance would have diminished even more. In any case focusing on these purposes undermined the one of helping impoverished people.

Propping up U.S. agriculture has motivated some foreign assistance. In 1954 Congress acted on the problem of vast food surpluses by approving Public Law 480. Under P.L. 480 food donations channeled abroad (much of it through voluntary relief agencies) have averaged about $240 million a year, and almost four times that amount in farm commodities have been sold on government-financed credit each year. But the purpose of combating hunger and malnutrition is secondary, mentioned by Congress in that legislative act only after it listed a prior purpose: "to develop and expand export markets for United States agricultural commodities." The subtitle of P.L. 480 describes it as: "An act to increase the consumption of United States agricultural commodities in foreign countries, to improve the foreign relations of the United States, and for other purposes." One of the "other purposes" is military—in 1971 most of the $310 million payable to us in foreign currency for food shipments was earmarked for South Vietnam's defense needs. But the law is tailored primarily for U.S. farms, especially large farms, an emphasis that shows up in more than $3 billion in cotton and tobacco that has been shipped abroad by the government under P.L. 480.

Over a third of American farm exports go to underdeveloped countries, but two-thirds of that amount is sold under special terms through our aid programs. This illustrates how one problem can be used to solve another, for U.S. food surpluses have helped millions of hungry people. But the P.L. 480 program has not always had the interest of recipient countries foremost in mind. Surpluses sometimes have been "dumped" abroad, a practice which benefits mainly U.S. farmers, but restricts and may depress the market for underdeveloped countries.

Providing markets for U.S. business has also influenced foreign assistance. In 1971, 99.7 percent of AID funds used to purchase products were spent in the United States, contrary to the widespread assumption that recipient nations shop around. When the foreign aid bill was temporarily scuttled that year, *The Wall Street Journal* headlined a story: "U.S. Firms Push to Get Aid Bill Resurrected; The Stakes: About $1 Billion in Annual Sales."

Foreign aid contains a natural element of benefit to U.S. business, since it stimulates trade. But not all businesses have been content to compete freely. Because of this, and in order to reduce slightly a U.S. balance-of-payments deficit, grants and loans have been "tied" to the purchase of U.S. products. *Forbes,* a business magazine, reported that our government put food shipments to India on a month-to-month basis until that country agreed to let Standard Oil of Indiana, which produces fertilizer in India, distribute and market that fertilizer at Standard's price. Later, in 1967, AID requested $50 million so that India could buy fertilizer, with the stated purpose of helping U.S. oil companies.

Aid-tying puts pressure on poor countries to import capital-intensive technology from us, since it is usually such imports that are covered by the terms of our assistance. The Foreign Assistance Act also requires that at least half of the tonnage financed by official U.S. loans or grants be carried on U.S. vessels, even though in some cases that more than doubles the shipping costs for underdeveloped countries. Tied aid runs counter to the idea of free-market competition, reflecting instead the kind of eighteenth-century British trade regulations to which the Thirteen Colonies objected.

The main way in which the original goal of economic assistance has been sidetracked for a secondary purpose is by using it to combat communism. In part this was deliberate, in part an accidental development. The Marshall Plan followed on the heels of the Truman Doctrine, which declared support for free people resisting internal or external aggression and was aimed immediately at communist threats within Greece and Turkey. So the Cold War played a prominent role from the start in the European Recovery Program.

Then in 1950, only 20 days after Congress enacted Truman's Point Four Program for aid to underdeveloped countries, the Korean War broke out. Defense against communism suddenly dominated the entire aid program.

We concentrated aid especially for South Korea, Formosa, and Indochina, apart from U.S. troop involvement. But elsewhere, too, aid flowed more abundantly to nations that stood militantly against communism. Neutral India, a parliamentary democracy with one-sixth of the world's population, received $1.8 billion in U.S. economic grants up to 1970, a figure almost identical to economic grants for tiny Taiwan, where Chiang imposed authoritarian (though economically progressive) rule upon the native Formosans. Even Pakistan, with its succession of military regimes, received more than four times as much from us in economic grants on a per capita basis than India did, most of that concentrated in West Pakistan, where a minority of the country's population lived. In addition we sent Pakistan an undisclosed amount of military assistance, an arsenal that it used not against a communist attack, but first against India in a fight over Kashmir, and later in the

1971 war against the East Pakistanis. As the case of Pakistan shows, such military assistance is more apt to be used in repressing internal challenges than in warding off aggression.

Consider the Alliance for Progress. From 1946 until President Kennedy initiated the Alliance in 1961, our development assistance grants to all of Latin America totaled less than $1.2 billion (compared to $1.6 billion for Taiwan during the same period). Then for a ten-year period beginning July, 1961, we averaged $418 million a year in grants and $506 million in loans. But even at the height of the Alliance, U.S. assistance to Latin America never equaled the profits that private U.S. investors earned there, and as Alliance funds shriveled, the gap widened.

Significantly, the Alliance was sold to Congress as a way of preventing Castro from exporting his revolution to other Latin countries. When that danger receded, so did interest in the Alliance.

President Kennedy had made clear that success of the Alliance hinged on democratic social reforms taking place. In announcing the Alliance he said, "This political freedom must be accompanied by social change. For unless necessary social reforms, including land and tax reform, are freely made—unless the great mass of Americans share in increasing prosperity—then our alliance, our revolution, our dream, and our freedom will fail." Soon after Kennedy's death, President Johnson put Thomas C. Mann in charge of the Alliance. Mann stressed protection of U.S. business investments and neutrality on social reforms. Assistance became a lever for occasional heavy-handed maneuvering on behalf of U.S. firms, a less than surprising development, since, as one analysis of the Alliance has pointed out, "business is the only interest group that consistently presents its viewpoint on Latin American affairs to U.S. government policy-makers." Social reforms faded. In Brazil's impoverished northeast, for example, the United States dropped support of a highly successful adult literacy program because the teaching method linked literacy with social and economic conditions, and generated demands for change.

The Alliance rapidly became just another unimaginative aid program. In Brazil a U.S. arrangement for immediate recognition and closer ties paved the way for a rightist military takeover there in 1964. Since then Brazil has received the largest share of U.S. assistance in Latin America, despite its suspension of constitutional rights and a pattern of repression and terror, including torture, which has been protested by the Roman Catholic Church and others. Consistent with this, the Rockefeller report in 1969 continued to view structural change in Latin America as a threat against which the United States must strengthen the hand of established, anticommunist rulers with increased military aid. The Alliance had lost its way.

As the example of Hitler shows, militant anticommunism and totalitarianism sometimes coincide. When in its fight against communism the United States lines up on the side of repressive powers, sensitive people in underdeveloped countries frequently conclude that the United States stands against justice and is abandoning its ideals.

The tapering off of assistance, together with its misapplication, indicates a monumental breakdown of leadership. On the occasion of his retirement late in 1972 Ambassador J. Robert Schaetzel, veteran U.S. diplomat, stated, "I am deeply disturbed about the way things are going. We . . . deserve better leaders no matter how bad we are as individuals." He said that the United States "no longer has a foreign policy strategy." For the past two decades our Presidents—with the general exception of John F. Kennedy—simply have not used the weight of their office to lay candidly and repeatedly before the public the desperate circumstances of hungry people or the meager amount of our assistance. Nor did any of them adequately sense the consequences of using foreign aid as a Cold War weapon. Congress—especially House members, who are accountable to the voters every two years—has been even more nearsighted. The House Foreign Affairs Committee still refuses to separate economic assistance from military assistance in submitting foreign aid legislation, because some committee members fear that economic assistance, considered alone by the full House, would be voted down.

If economic assistance has been inadequate, and if it has been pushed and pulled to serve purposes other than that of spurring development in the poor countries, then failure should not surprise us. *The requirements call for generosity on our part and for a program of assistance that is rationally designed to bring about economic development.* The U.S. public can come to understand why success has been limited, and can then insist on an imaginative approach to world development—not because this step will produce a utopia, but because without that step we may produce quite the opposite.

These changes are essential:

1. *Economic assistance can be separated from military assistance and calculated accurately for the public.* This separation has been only partly accomplished. The two forms of aid could be so clearly divorced that even the press would not combine them in one headline. Furthermore, the figure of economic assistance should be stripped of its padding. In these ways the public could see accurately for the first time the microscopic size of our assistance.

2. *Economic assistance can be more nearly separated from considerations of international politics and private domestic interests.* The 1970 report of the Presidential Task Force on International Development said that helping people build an equitable political and economic order "should be a cardinal aim of U.S. foreign policy," but it also warned: "This country should not look for gratitude or votes, or any specific short-term foreign policy gains from our participation in international development."

The same report added: "Neither can [the United States] assume that development will necessarily bring stability. Development implies change—political and social, as well as economic—and such change, for a time, may be disruptive." We cannot predict with assurance the political outcome of development efforts, nor can we expect countries always to choose or acquire governments of our liking. Gains and setbacks will continue to occur. We can respect others even when they differ with us, however, and have some confidence that within the context of peaceful development, freedom has its best chance, and probably its only chance, of prevailing.

3. *We can insist that better criteria be established for recipients of economic assistance.* Assistance will have the best chance of spurring development if it is given not only on the basis of need, but also in response to the willingness of recipient countries to bring about reforms essential for development. The main problem in the past with attaching conditions and goals to aid has been that the conditions and goals attached were often incompatible with the needs of development. The president of a Latin American nation told me in 1971 that the chief complaint among progressive leaders of the developing nations is not that the United States tries to dictate terms for its assistance, but that the United States is not really interested in their development. When lack of interest is combined with conditions on aid that diminish its usefulness, resentment naturally follows.

4. *Economic assistance can be carried out primarily through international agencies.* President Truman's Point Four proposal urged that assistance to underdeveloped countries "be a cooperative enterprise in which all nations work together through the United Nations and its specialized agencies whenever practicable." International agencies offer the most dependable method of removing assistance from the service of our own economic or political interests. Although international sponsors are also subject to national interests, pressures are held in check somewhat under such sponsorship. These agencies also are in a better position to monitor conditions by which countries qualify for aid. But they do need to increase their efficiency and capacity.

5. *The United States can lead the way in generously supporting assistance for development.* Such leadership is an essential way of exercising global responsibility, and it reflects the growing eco-

nomic capacity of our country. Effective development cannot take place unless it is adequately financed. Some argue that we should first take care of our neglected domestic problems—the cities, rural and urban poverty, hunger, housing, jobs, and schools. Gunnar Myrdal has pointed out that the United States is not as rich as Americans generally believe.

> In an international comparison its wealth and national income have to be decreased very substantially by what I call its "debt to the [U.S.] poor," which must be paid if the nation is not going to disintegrate or become a police state. This debt . . . is much bigger than is commonly accounted by Americans.
>
> Some of the most advanced Western nations probably are now as rich as the United States, primarily because they have never put themselves in such a debt, or, if they did, paid it long ago. . . .

This granted, the United States will come off "relatively very rich" in Myrdal's judgment, fully capable of responding in its tradition of generosity to global poverty.

Should the United States adopt as an assistance target the 1 percent of Gross National Product so widely suggested for the rich nations? That target would be a substantial step ahead; but it is still timid, primarily because those who discuss it usually include private investment and sometimes military support, as well as official assistance, while the last is fatly padded to distort upward its actual value. I have already indicated that if official U.S. economic assistance were figured on a reasonably accurate basis, it would amount to more than one-tenth of 1 percent of our Gross National Product.

/I propose that we accept 1 percent as the target for official assistance, but count it honestly. Thus the tying of aid, if not eliminated, would have to be acknowledged by listing the aid with an appropriate reduction of value. We would count loans on the basis of their concessional worth only—or at full value *minus* repayments, with interest, on previous loans. With such straight-forward accounting, adoption of the 1 percent target would multiply tenfold present U.S. economic assistance. A national output of $1.2 trillion would, for example, yield real annual assistance of $12 billion.

That does not mean we should stop at 1 percent—or even start there. Sweden provides an illuminating example. Once low among rich nations in percentage of assistance, the Swedish parliament decided in 1968 to increase its aid each year by 25 percent until in fiscal year 1974–75 it reaches 1 percent of its output; and already a considerable opinion favors continuation of the increase above that level. Following this pattern, the United States might pledge immediately to raise its assistance by one-tenth of 1 percent each year until the full 1 percent goal has been reached, with occasion for review at that point. This gradual approach could be a way of acknowledging the nation's commitment to resolve within a decade its most pressing and postponed domestic problems. It would place assistance on a more sure footing than annual political whims allow.

Whether financing development in this way is foolish or sensible depends on our values. Here is India: almost one-sixth of the human race, miserably poor, struggling against frightful odds, but peaceful and democratic. What is India worth to us? What are we going to do? How much will we offer in national resources to see hundreds of millions of Indians move toward minimal human decency and away from catastrophe?

Perhaps little or nothing. There is a curious agreement between obdurate conservatives and some spokesmen on the left which sees no good emerging from U.S. attempts to help—right-wingers, because such efforts contradict a dog-eat-dog type of free enterprise; leftists, in part at least because Lenin's revision of Marx argued that wealthy capitalistic nations were driven by necessity of their own survival to exploit underdeveloped countries. Fortunately most of us subscribe to neither version of "reality."

More serious resistance will come from those who maintain that "we can't afford it." It must be candidly acknowledged that even a small "development tax" on our national output would shift some emphasis away from unrestrained consumption. In this sense it would be felt by every citizen, though the rate of economic growth is such that the impact would be minimal. Robert McNamara told the 1972 annual meeting of the World Bank:

Projected to the end of the century—only a generation away—the people of the developed countries will be enjoying per capita incomes in 1972 prices of more than $8,000 a year, while the masses of the poor (who by that time will total over two and one-quarter billion) will on average receive less than $200 per capita, and some 800 million of these will receive less than $100. . . .

The rich nations are not being asked to diminish their riches in order to help the poor nations. They are only asked to share a tiny percentage of their continually increasing wealth.

This would not have to make a single person poorer. Compassion and justice are not profit-making enterprises, of course. They are costly, and their costs have to be absorbed by the community— in this case partly by the community of rich nations. But the cost has to be tallied against the cost of not doing it—like the problems that have accumulated in our cities, which never went into anyone's bookkeeping, and now turn up compounded with decades of usurious interest. We have been "saving" money the way a homeowner saves by not painting his house, not patching the roof, or not fixing a broken furnace. In a similar way we can "save" money by not spending it on urgent world needs; but the real cost of such thrift should be tallied in terms of human suffering, international discord, arms races, violence, and depressed economies. *A war against hunger is cheaper than a war against people, and a race against poverty costs less than an armaments race.*

If Asians, Africans, and Latins lift themselves out of poverty it would, in the long run, work to the economic benefit of everyone. As John F. Kennedy said, "The rising tide lifts all the boats." The United States has demonstrated again and again that when the poor advance, they stimulate the entire economy. There is an international parallel: as poor countries develop, they become better U.S. customers.

The present period will be decisive for this nation, because the war in Vietnam has compelled us to reexamine our foreign policy. Unfortunately, indications of a turning inward after Vietnam are evident. In 1971 President Nixon said, "Our foreign policy today steers a steady course between the past danger of overinvolvement and the new temptation of underinvolvement." The President was right in citing the danger of underinvolvement, but wrong in failing to discern a far more central question: what *kind* of involvement should this be?

Leadership will be crucial. In 1971 while Nixon was seeking cutbacks in economic assistance, he warned against "growing and disturbing isolationism." Less than two months later he told the U.S. Chamber of Commerce, "What we need today is to take a lot more pride in the system that has made it possible for us to be the most generous and the most compassionate nation, not only to our own people but to other people on the face of the earth." The audience cheered. We do have some traits of generosity to build on, but inflated self-congratulations deceive rather than lead, particularly when they occur in the face of a patently stingy performance.

Without distinguished leadership the United States is certain to turn inward. But if leaders are willing to inform the public and enlist support, a global program enabling people all over the world to begin working their way out of hunger and poverty could become a fundamental national goal.

16

Let Them Eat Missiles

By an excessive reliance on military power the United States has reduced its capacity to assist underdeveloped countries. As long as the politics of power rather than the politics of justice dominate our foreign policy, and until the Department of Defense ceases to corner a disproportionate share of the budget, we will do too little toward eliminating poverty in our own country, much less deal with it on a worldwide basis.

By itself, however, reducing military appropriations will not guarantee one additional penny for poverty. Vietnam has taught us that. Those who said, "If we wind down the war, we can start solving our urban problems," proved to be wrong. Lack of will, more than the cost of Vietnam, prevented us from solving those problems. The war, tragically, was just easier to get appropriations for. As our troops returned, tax reductions rather than other needs claimed first attention; and defense spending continues to rise.

This nation's defense requirements are admittedly enormous and costly. Given the stance of present Soviet leadership, acknowledging the need for reasonable power-balancing, and taking into account the soaring costs of both nuclear and nonnuclear technology, our military spending will be high. But we have exceeded the limits of reason. We depend too much on raw power and pay too little attention to the exercise of power through justice.

Consider that:

1. *The cost of the arms race is out of hand.* In 1961, shortly after he retired from the presidency, Dwight D. Eisenhower said at the Naval War College:

. . . We know that the Communists seek to break the economy of the United States—an economy that is based on free enterprise and sound currency. If we, therefore, put one more dollar in a weapons system than we should, we are weakening the defense of the United States.

While more than a sound economy is at stake in military spending, Eisenhower's misgiving was well placed, because most of the deficit in our inflationary federal budget can be accounted for by excessive defense spending.

Military overspend has only one virtue: it creates jobs. But it does so at an exorbitant cost; and, like building pyramids, it constitutes a dead-end use of resources, stimulating neither long-range economic gains nor adding to the quality of life. It results in a substantial increase each year in the amount of the budget that goes for interest rather than for goods and services, thus obligating future federal administrations for immense expenditures over which they have no control. As I write this, for example, the federal deficit projected for fiscal year 1973 appears to be nearly $30 billion. The interest alone on that amount will be almost $2 billion each succeeding year. That is a continuing obligation (apart from the repayment of principal) which the federal government assumes. For fiscal year 1974 the federal budget will have to be about $2 billion extra, not for social improvements, but merely to take care of those increased interest payments. So the costs are twofold in the defense field: an immediate absorption, and a commitment to interest costs in the future regardless of later defense expenditures. The interest cost is paid by taxpayers to those who hold government bonds, so it is not "lost," but it does constitute a redistribution of income that favors the wealthy.

From the end of World War II to June, 1972, this country spent $1.3 trillion ($1.3 thousand billion) on defense. The budget for fiscal year 1973 shows about 35 cents of every tax dollar going for defense and military assistance abroad. If we include veterans' benefits and interest on the national debt, most of which pays for past wars, almost half of the national budget goes for defense purposes. The percentage for defense has been steadily declining, but in actual amounts it is on the rise.

Staggering as the sums spent for the arms race are in themselves, the peril they represent can best be measured by comparisons. Worldwide military expenditures which reached $216 billion in 1971 *exceed the total income of the poorer half of the world.* Contrasting that sum with the aid given to underdeveloped countries, Robert S. McNamara called it "the mark of an ultimate, and I sometimes fear, incurable folly."

The United States devours over $215 million a day for military purposes. Every 14 hours the Department of Defense outspends the entire annual budget of the UN World Food Program. In the same 14 hours it spends more than the World Health Organization and the Food and Agriculture Organization combined. It takes the Department of Defense a mere 30 hours to consume what the UN Development Program uses in a year. The United States allocates about 60 times more for current military purposes than it does for economic assistance. U.S. officials excuse our poor record in aid-giving on the basis of this extraordinary military outlay—our "far heavier share of the common defense burden," in the words of President Nixon's Task Force on International Development. But this is a let-them-eat-missiles policy.

The only U.S. government agency that concerns itself with weapons reduction is the Arms Control and Disarmament Agency. It operates with an annual budget of approximately $10 million.

By comparison, the Department of Defense budgets nearly a thousand times that much each year just on research, and roughly nineteen times that amount for public relations.

From 1963 to 1972 the federal government spent $686 billion for defense—several billion *more* than its entire collection of individual income taxes during the same period. The 1973 appropriations of $78.8 billion for U.S. military programs amounts to an average cost of $1,500 for a family of four, quite apart from interest payments (another $400) or veterans' benefits ($224). In effect every man, woman and child in this country pays the federal government approximately:

> $375 for current military needs
> 33 for education
> 19 for job training and employment services
> 24 for housing and community development
> 12 for natural resources and the environment
> 6 for economic assistance to the hungry nations

Several presidential commissions investigating causes of our domestic crisis have cited long neglect of such things as decent housing, and jobs for the unemployed; but the nation's budget continues to ignore these almost self-evident conclusions—especially ironic since the Commission on Violence, headed by Dr. Milton B. Eisenhower, held that the security of the nation is threatened more by internal social disorders than by external enemies. In short, excess military spending represents annually millions of man-years of labor that could be used at home and abroad to build a more humane way of life. Instead it gets sucked into the arms race.

When we ask *why* this waste occurs, formidable witnesses speak up. Stuart Symington, former Secretary of the Air Force and the only U.S. Senator serving on both the Armed Services and the Foreign Affairs Committees, says that we could cut the cost of defense spending by one-fourth or more by withdrawing from half of our major military bases abroad and by eliminating duplica-

tions caused by interservice rivalry. According to Robert S. Mc-
Namara, Secretary of Defense under Presidents Kennedy and
Johnson, "My problem was never to get sufficient money for de-
fense, but, rather, to avoid buying weapons that weren't needed."

2. *The military-industrial complex has gained too much influence.* In his farewell message to Congress, President Eisenhower
warned:

> In the councils of government we must guard against the acquisition
> of unwarranted influence, whether sought or unsought, by the military-
> industrial complex. The potential for the disastrous rise of misplaced
> power exists and will persist. We must never let the weight of this com-
> bination endanger our liberties or democratic processes. We should never
> take anything for granted.

The new U.S. experience of an immense military establishment has
had a "total influence—economic, political, even spiritual," Eisenhower said, and added that it was felt at every level of government. He sensed no diabolical plot, or even, he implied, an evil
intention—for the danger exists whether the influence is "sought
or unsought." When the military and industrial sectors serve their
acknowledged functions, they automatically exercise an enormous
power that generates its own momentum. Too few are knowledge-
able enough in military affairs to counterbalance their requests.

A military leader, trained to cope with the threat of attack, must
plan for the worst possible contingencies. He must suspect an
adversary's motives at all times, and is tempted, by nature of his
responsibility, to exaggerate the enemy's capabilities. Unless it is
carefully controlled, this process may break down rather than build
the nation's security. McNamara has reflected:

> We, for instance, didn't plan to have the numerical advantage that we
> had in 1966 or 1967 *vis-à-vis* the Soviets. We didn't need it. The reason
> we had it was this range of uncertainty that one must guard against, and
> there's no other way to guard against it than by, in a sense, assuming the
> worst and acting accordingly. Then, when the worst doesn't happen,
> you've got more than you need, and that's bad enough. But worse than

that is the fact that they see you have it, and they react, and then you've got to do it again. And that's exactly what happened. That's what causes escalation; that is what makes it so dangerous.

President Nixon's blue-ribbon Defense Panel concluded that neither the President nor the Secretary of Defense has a staff competent to evaluate recommendations of the Joint Chiefs of Staff or of field commanders. This crucial gap in civilian control constitutes, as the panel said, a "high risk" to the nation.

Unnecessary secrecy by the executive branch concerning military operations also hampers civilian control. According to Senator Symington, it jeopardizes "not only the welfare and prosperity of the United States but also, and most significantly, the national security." Our military activities abroad, he maintains, are far better known by adversaries than by the U.S. public, and sometimes even by Congress itself. Almost a year before the Pentagon Papers became public, Symington wrote that secrecy "has now developed to a point where military activities often first create and then dominate foreign policy responses."

If military leaders tend to gather undue influence, so do leaders of industry. Like the military, industry finds itself spilling into a forbidden area only by doing well what it is expected to do. Anxious to develop and sell its products to a good customer (the U.S. government), industry pushes the arms race by acting toward the government the way it acts toward any other big customer. The fact that each contract means jobs and taxes in some congressman's district gives defense industries considerable leverage.

The government has been a generous customer. In 1970 the General Accounting Office reported that an analysis of 146 defense contracts showed an average pretax profit on total capital investment of 28.3 percent, or roughly twice the normal average for manufacturing profits. Senator Paul Douglas pointed out inefficiency and excess profiteering in the defense industry for more than a decade, but no one listened to him until McNamara was named Secretary of Defense. This inefficiency and profiteering feeds the cost of the arms race, and it also encourages contractors to invent military improvements and promote their wares—which puts them in the business of trying to influence policy.

The effort, technology, and money that go into war preparations are matched, astonishingly, by almost no preparation for peace. In 1970 Senator Abraham Ribicoff's Senate Subcommittee on Executive Reorganization and Governmental Research sent out a questionnaire to 118 major industries, 18 big-city mayors, and seven labor leaders regarding preparations for conversion of industry from wartime to peacetime. Senator Ribicoff summarized the findings this way:

In general, the responses indicated that private industry is not interested in initiating any major attempts at meeting critical public needs. Most industries have no plans or projects designed to apply their resources to civilian problems. Furthermore, they indicated an unwillingness to initiate such actions without a firm commitment from the Government that their efforts will quickly reap the financial rewards to which they are accustomed. Otherwise, they appear eager to pursue greater defense contracts or stick to commercial products within the private sector.

The government freely plans and subsidizes inflationary war preparations, but is afraid to plan and subsidize a noninflationary peace. By defaulting on that responsibility the government makes itself vulnerable to the unwarranted influence of the military-industrial complex.

3. *We have long ago passed the point of nuclear overkill.* In 1972, when President Nixon signed the Strategic Arms Limitation Treaty with the Soviet Union, the world's nuclear stockpile exceeded 50,000 megatons (equal to 50 billion tons of TNT), or the equivalent of almost 15 tons of TNT for every man, woman, and child on earth—and 60 tons per person for the NATO and Warsaw Pact nations combined. According to one estimate, the United States could wipe out Soviet population and industrial centers of more than 100,000 people 34 times, while the Soviet Union could destroy ours 13 times.

"Overkill" is the word that has emerged from this nightmare of competition. Each side has the capability of wiping out his opponent many times over, even if one concedes the destruction of most missiles before they are launched as a result of a first strike by the enemy, and adds to that a generous number of failures. The irony is that either side requires only one thing: enough nuclear retaliatory power to discourage the other from striking first. How much power would that be? Probably the mere likelihood that several nuclear warheads would reach their target. But both the Soviet Union and the United States are far beyond that point.

How do we account for the impulses that prompt nations to successively higher and more sophisticated levels of overkill? At the root may be simply the instinct that you have to get ahead of the enemy because "more powerful means more safe." Although the SALT agreements signed in Moscow froze the number of offensive missiles permitted for either side, it did not limit the number of nuclear warheads, or the development of more sophisticated nuclear technology. Setting quantitative limits for missiles was a major step forward, but it allowed the arms race to continue at full speed in other ways, and even prompted the Administration to ask for special increases in defense spending.

Any worthwhile steps toward defusing nuclear antagonism involve hidden risks, but not nearly the risk of continuing an arms race that mires both the United States and the Soviet Union more deeply in nuclear terror, increasing their power and paradoxically decreasing the security of both.

4. *The poor nations, too, are engaged in an arms race—and we are supplying arms.* Their military spending has risen even more rapidly, on a percentage basis, than has that of the rich nations. The supply of weapons to poor nations multiplied by more than seven between 1950 and 1970. In a recent three-year period, Egypt spent over two-thirds of its domestic fixed investments on the military. For fiscal year 1973 the Pakistani government, despite heralded social reforms, allocated $405 million for defense from a total national budget of $608 million. By comparison $20 million was

marked for a "massive program of low-cost housing and environmental improvement."

The United States leads competitors for the lucrative arms
market, having sold over $2 billion worth of military hardware in
1971, with the Soviet Union and European countries also deeply
involved.

The underdeveloped regions need less, not more, spending on
arms, so the assumption ought to be against such traffic rather than
for it. The argument, "If we don't sell it to them, somebody else
will," sounds too much like the excuse of a narcotics racketeer. The
United States should scale down its participation in the poor
nations' arms race and press instead for an international "small
SALT" (small-arms limitation treaty) as a follow-up of the
nonproliferation treaty of 1968 which bans the spread of nuclear
weapons to other nations.

5. *We have overextended our military presence abroad*. The
war in Vietnam dramatizes this overextension most vividly, but
even apart from Indochina the U.S. military establishment spreads
far and wide. In 1969 Defense Secretary Laird said, ". . . We've
had some 15,000 [nuclear] warheads stored all over the world for
the last 10 years . . . ," although not even Congress knows where
they are. In 1972 the Pentagon put the number of U.S. military
bases scattered around the globe (excluding U.S. territory, Thailand, and Vietnam) at 367. This formidable global military
presence stands behind the impression that the United States wants
to police the world.

Regardless of the justification for garrisoning our troops
throughout the world after World War II—and I believe most of
it was fundamentally justified—these forces now should be
sharply reduced. Neither our defense nor the protection of treaty
nations requires us to maintain this network.

Our overextended military presence gives an unnecessary impression that the United States wants to dominate the world. That
is its most deplorable aspect, but not the only one. From 1951 to
1953 I served as a soldier in Western Europe. At that time our

presence was necessary, and Europeans accepted the fact. But even then it did not require a formal education to realize that foreign troops in any country cannot avoid causing considerable resentment, though much of it may go unspoken. Imagine how we would feel if our nation, or even the town we live in, had large numbers of German troops stationed in it on a more or less permanent basis. I mention this because it is part—small but not insignificant—of the reason troops should be stationed abroad only when they are absolutely essential. U.S. troops are, in general, like troops of any nation stationed abroad. Lonesome and unhappy, many try to solve their emotional problems with drinking and social outlets not appreciated by most local residents. The U.S. soldier presents a bigger problem than a soldier of another nation because ours is paid much more, and therefore has more money for heavy drinking, visiting prostitutes, and other excesses. Not all GIs are guilty of antisocial behavior, of course; many have founded orphanages or done other acts of courage and compassion. Yet a U.S. military base in another nation obviously creates more ill will than friends.

U.S. military missions and counterinsurgency efforts in Latin American countries provide a less visible but no less offensive presence. This program includes research, training, and equipment for military and police officers in most Latin American countries, as well as the intelligence network of the CIA. Counterinsurgency is a legitimate domestic concern, especially where there are high levels of social unrest and the possibility of communist exploitation. Unfortunately—and I speak as a former member of the Counter Intelligence Corps—counterinsurgency programs tend to nourish exaggerated fears, and in Latin America it has not been possible to keep such U.S. programs from strengthening regressive and undemocratic forces in a number of countries.

Perhaps because of this, the opinion has swept through Latin America that U.S. military intrigue and CIA agents lurk everywhere, conniving to expose and destroy movements of social reform. The military in a free country is one part of the delicate balance between liberty and security. In the United States our tradition of liberty is strong enough so that the military does not present a great danger to freedom. But that is not the case in most nations. The people of Brazil, where the largest U.S. military mission has operated, widely blame the United States—rightly or wrongly—for the most repressive features of that country's military dictatorship. It is almost beside the point to argue about the extent to which these U.S. military projects have been misunderstood. It is enough to realize that today they arouse hostility toward our country and in many cases undermine our goals.

Since the end of the Korean War, excessive reliance on military power has served to frustrate hopes for world development and has backed the United States away from its ideals. In the underdeveloped countries, above all, our foreign policy has floundered. A decade ago our relationship with Latin America, though under fire, was still marked by good will. Before the 1960s were finished much of that had been used up, and Governor Rockefeller faced hostile crowds everywhere on his fact-finding trip through the region. Indochina in particular taught us the cost and futility of forcing our will against a strong, nationalist—albeit communist and totalitarian—movement.

Russia and China, too, learned through painful setbacks of their own that attempts to foment uprisings in underdeveloped countries were not working.

The major powers will have to bid for influence primarily in the marketplaces of example and assistance, rather than through the use of muscle; and they will bid for it without being able to control countries, for the latter increasingly reject a role of dependency. The United States can welcome this situation, because the spirit of national independence within these countries coincides with our own tradition of nonintervention—a stronger heritage of ours than the exceptions may lead people to believe. It also harmonizes with our having championed the principle of self-determination since World War I. We have reason to hope that developing countries will be more favorably disposed toward democracy if we are partners with them in working to eliminate hunger and poverty.

Because some internal conflict and even occasional small wars seem certain to accompany development, proponents of development who expect an immediate "peace dividend" would be well advised to take a more modest view. For the short run, development could bring additional strife. For the long run, however, a world in which hunger, poverty, and inequalities are allowed to worsen cannot be peaceful, if indeed it can survive. By working together for the common good, nations can gradually create a climate which diminishes violence as an acceptable method of solving problems. With the long view in mind, then, we can say with Pope Paul that "the new name for peace is development."

Less than two months after he became President, Dwight D. Eisenhower said, "Every gun that is made, every warship launched, every rocket fired signifies, in the final sense, a theft from those who hunger and are not fed, those who are cold and are not clothed." A more judicious use of power would help to reverse this "theft from those who hunger" by releasing many billions of dollars each year for peaceful development.

Part IV

A PROGRAM
FOR ACTION

1973 Paul Simon
the politics of world hunger

17

Proposal for Global Development

Economic development should be shaped primarily to help people out of hunger and poverty, not to make the world a carbon copy of the United States. Too often development has meant establishing the apparatus for producing and consuming nonessentials at an ever-accelerating pace in imitation of rich northern nations. Development in this sense can justly be condemned, both because it does violence to cultures and social values that should be preserved, and even more because it promotes islands of extravagance among people who are basically destitute. In the words of Denis Goulet, a specialist in development ethics, "To pursue the development dream of general affluence . . . is to condemn most men to frustration and to exacerbate existing inequalities in the Third World."

Because poor people, like everyone else, measure themselves largely in relation to their surroundings, their condition is felt more acutely when prosperity is flaunted and at the same time denied them. Consequently a type of development which spreads inequalities and fails to move the mass of poor people upward becomes increasingly less tolerable.

197

/Can we equate the affluent life with the good life? Is it not possible that underdeveloped countries may favor other goals over the pursuit of affluence and as a result demonstrate preferable alternatives? Beyond enabling people to eat adequately, to work, and to obtain basic medical and material requirements for life, we should begin to think of development less in terms of accelerated production and consumption, and more in terms of human qualities that enrich people in other ways/I apply this principle to our own country, first of all. But it has a particular application to underdeveloped countries, most of which cannot hope, perhaps ever, to produce and consume as audaciously as the United States now does.

A country in which health centers are available for all is more developed than one with a higher per capita ratio of physicians and hospitals, if these serve only the well-to-do. A country with beaches and parks for the public can be judged wealthier than one in which superior natural facilities are cornered by a minority of property owners. A country in which villagers work together to build roads, schools, and cottage industries may be more advanced than one concentrating on steel mills and engineers. This approach is important, for even without trying to mimic our habits of consumption, it will be enormously difficult for underdeveloped countries to wipe out hunger and to overcome the most fundamental liabilities of poverty.

/Because that struggle is at best long and arduous, development should not be inflated with expectations that are likely to mislead people both in the poor nations and in assisting countries. The frustration and disillusion that result can only undermine development. A timetable for achieving the elementary goals of eliminating hunger and poverty will stretch over decades, probably well past our lifetimes, even with an unprecedented international effort toward this end./

ARRANGING
A LIVABLE
WORLD

What kind of world do we want to build, not just in the fantasy land of idle dreams, but with practical efforts? If we envision a world that does not ask annoying questions or demand much of us, then the idea of a major, cohesive strategy for world development sounds hopelessly utopian. On the other hand, if as a nation we seek a world in which even the poor are able to work and eat and live on at least a minimally decent level, a world that in the long run has a reasonable chance of holding together with its humanity intact, then an expanded program for development is practical. /

/Without minimizing the monumental accomplishments of the past 25 years, it is fair to say that present efforts in development are much too limited and uneven. Neglect, overlapping, projects left dangling because the mood of Congress changes, or because a new administration is elected—these happen too frequently and they *contribute* to hunger and poverty. The facts argue convincingly for international development on a scale that corresponds to world needs, and sufficiently coordinated so as to embody a truly integrated, global approach./

/We have already carried out massive, coordinated efforts in other areas: the NASA space program, war mobilizations, and international industrial corporations. As models for development their usefulness is limited because they operate with a high degree of precision in methods, as well as in goals, while development is saturated with social issues and questions of value that are far more complex and slippery/ Nevertheless these examples do give us an idea of what we can accomplish, on an exceedingly large and comprehensive scale, once we have decided to do so. If a conservative like Spiro Agnew favors "total environmental planning" to solve the nation's domestic problems, as he did in an interview with James Reston, then on what basis other than our own nearsightedness can a similar approach be faulted for the world as a whole?/

To begin with, international development calls for an enormous concentration of brain power. Michael Harrington, whose *Other America* has been credited with spurring the War on Poverty ~~of the early 1960s~~, was hired as a consultant for the group that drew up the Economic Opportunity Act of 1964. Harrington says he became conscious of the fact that the intellectual deficit was greater than the financial one. Members of the task force were dedicated and often brilliant. "Yet all of us suffered from the fact that, during the Eisenhower years, few people had thought of what to do about poverty. When the moment for action finally came, practical men were hamstrung because not enough visionaries had preceded them." The War on Poverty, because it parallels more nearly the present limitations of assistance, is hardly a useful model for the development efforts that I am proposing. However, the deficit Harrington noted suggests the intellectual resources that a global war on poverty will have to marshal.

Fortunately we do not have to start from scratch, because nations and international agencies have accumulated experience for more than two and a half decades. We can begin at once to intensify development in every country, and feed the knowledge we accumulate into an information storage and retrieval system. The important thing is to move forward on the basis of discernible opportunities that already exist in abundance. We will enlarge our understanding in the process, and be better equipped to offer a plausible vision worthy of international response. People will be summoned to support global development not when they hear proposals that are geared cautiously to existing political trends, but when they see a clear picture of the world and understand the likely consequences of various responses to it.

The international community can expand present development efforts, with emphasis on the following:

Labor-intensive production. More assistance is needed for development programs that create productive employment for large numbers of unemployed workers, primarily in rural areas but also in the cities. There is enough to be done in underdeveloped countries to occupy every able-bodied person, but the task of preparing and organizing people for this is incredibly difficult/ China offers the most astounding example to date, but with an authoritarian efficiency that no noncommunist country is prepared to duplicate. /The challenge of putting everyone to work for the common good deserves top priority as a development goal. This could turn out to be crucial in the struggle against hunger./

Production and distribution of food. /World development requires poor countries to become as sufficient as possible in food, so that each country not only maximizes its productive capacity, but fits its productivity into a sensible global pattern. The aim should be wider consumption of food among the poor, along with increased opportunities, especially for the rural poor, to improve their living standards/ It makes little sense for agricultural-surplus countries like the United States, Canada, and France to let food production be determined by subsidies rather than by needs. Among the distortions that result, some food products get marketed at unnecessarily high prices, and others at artificially low prices. This approach is costly for the producing country and harmful to poor nations./ As a general rule, developing countries should be encouraged to specialize in farm products they are best suited to produce, so countries like our own can concentrate more on filling the vital gaps./

/The problem of food surpluses in a hungry world is essentially a contradiction. The solution, however, has to be far more sophisticated than simply shipping overseas as large a supply of commodities as we possibly can—a practice that could ruin farmers in the poor countries/ /As it increases food production, the world can rationalize its marketing and distribution so that benefits are spread everywhere, but with the poor countries foremost in mind. This would include increasing storage of commodities under international auspices (buying in fat years and selling in lean years), providing proteins free or at low cost to pregnant or nursing mothers and to young children, and expanding food-for-work projects./

Technology. /Research and technology should serve the poor, but instead they overwhelmingly benefit rich nations. The United States, for example, has spent hundreds of millions of dollars to develop substitutes for such products as cocoa, coffee, rubber, and fibers, while the countries adversely affected by these substitutes spend virtually nothing to plan or develop alternatives. The 1973 U.S. budget calls for $18 billion in research and development, most of it for military purposes. Including also private funds, this country lays out 30 times as much for research as the entire poor world does. Any one of the top U.S. corporations probably spends more on research than do all the developing nations of any single continent.

The "brain drain," which annually brings thousands of scientists, professors, physicians, and engineers to the rich nations from poor countries, illustrates the inverted logic of concentrating technology where it is least needed. The Pearson commission reported that in 1967 underdeveloped countries "obtained the temporary services of 16,000 foreign advisors . . . but the UN estimates that close to 40,000 of their own national professionals emigrated to the industrialized countries." By 1970 approximately one-third of the physicians starting practice in the United States were immigrants trained abroad. In 1972 nearly 5,000 physicians immigrated to the United States from Asia alone.

There is a further irony. Although India loses about a third of its graduating medical students, an example of that country's contribution to the brain drain, it would be incapable of employing its educated citizens even if they returned from abroad in large numbers, so poor are these countries, and so mismatched is technology to their needs. This points also to an *internal* brain drain, which diverts some of the most talented youth away from local problems and prepares them instead for lucrative positions abroad —a form of development assistance in reverse.

A comprehensive plan for world development would clearly embody a coordinated effort to put technology at the service of the world's poor. They do not need Western technology transferred to them lock, stock, and barrel as much as they need the development of alternate technologies which are applicable to non-Western situations, especially labor-intensive improvements. In many areas this will mean starting from scratch to devise entirely new approaches, in order to involve and assist rather than bypass the poor. /

Trade and investment. Present economic theory governing international trade emerged during the period of colonialism. It tends to obscure the problems of underdeveloped countries by assuming that there is a harmony of interests in trade which works toward the gradual equalization of profits. That assumption stands against all experience, according to Gunnar Myrdal: "The fact is that, contrary to that theory, international trade—and capital movements—will generally tend to breed inequality, and will do so the more strongly when substantial inequalities are already established."/

The failure of the international trade organizations (the International Monetary Fund and the General Agreement on Tariffs and Trade) to counteract this inequality prompted underdeveloped countries to have the United Nations establish the UN Conference on Trade and Development. But UNCTAD assemblies in 1964, 1968, and again in 1972 left the poor countries frustrated, especially on the crucial issue of obtaining more markets in the industrialized nations, and also on questions of monetary reform and debt relief. /

/ Large international companies are likewise causing more and more concern because of their ability to fix prices and control economies. In fact, as ITT efforts to prevent a duly-elected Chilean government from taking office illustrate, these companies can exercise improper and disproportionate political influence as well. A global development program should include proposals for protecting countries from abuses by large international corporations, through tools such as international antitrust legislation, to cite a possible example./

On the more positive side, proposals should also be put forward for inducing a greater flow of beneficial private investments to poor countries. This assumes adequate safeguards against some of the pitfalls I have cited in previous chapters.

International financing. Comprehensive global development calls for financing on a much more generous scale than we have seen so far. Ironically, we do not know how much capital could be effectively used, because we have never engaged in or even planned development on a sufficiently large scale. At what point does the infusion of money touch off inflationary spirals in a poor nation? How should development efforts be organized efficiently and co-ordinated? While these questions clearly imply that development financing has limits in terms of effective results, the danger is not overfunding, but vastly inadequate funding. Answers can only be worked out in the context of expanded international development.

One important method of financing development concerns the use of Special Drawing Rights. SDRs are "paper gold" credits that increase international monetary reserves, by simple international agreement, for the purpose of financing trade. SDRs were first issued in 1970, and by spring of 1972, $9.5 billion in SDRs had been created, but three-fourths of it had gone to the rich nations, with the United States the chief beneficiary. Future issues should go primarily to the underdeveloped countries. That would give those countries a substantial boost, and because they do most of their trading with rich nations, it offers clear benefits to the U.S. economy.

Like SDRs, the exploitation of the ocean beds has immense long-range implications for the ability of poor countries to finance their development. If the ocean floor is to be used peacefully for the benefit of all mankind, the proceeds drawn from it should be shared on the basis of country population.

Logic also moves us toward the establishment of some form of international income tax. The practice of taxing people on the basis of their ability to pay, in order to promote the common good, is a relatively recent one. In the United States, Congress enacted the first permanent income tax in 1913, and the meager beginnings of social security in 1935, only a few years prior to World War II. Naturally, when governments did not consider themselves responsible for promoting internal development by this method, doing so for colonial possessions or countries abroad never occurred to them. But with the principle of progressive taxation well established and its benefits widely acknowledged, it makes sense to apply that principle to the problem of international inequalities. Robert McNamara contends, "We must apply at the world level that same sharing of wealth, that same standard of justice and compassion, without which our own national societies would surely fall apart." Earlier Pope Paul stated that "the superfluous wealth of rich countries should be placed at the service of poor nations, the rule which up to now held good for the benefit of those nearest to us, must today be applied to all the needy of the world."

Doing so would mean removing official assistance from the arena of private charity, with all the imbalances and the emotional corrosion it entails for both donors and recipients, and arranging it instead on the basis of treaties. This method would emphasize partnership and underscore the fact that nations help each other through development. Earlier I suggested 1 percent of the national output as a foreseeable target, to be calculated not by inflated arithmetic, but on the basis of actual hardcore assistance. If the target were reached gradually, say over a period of a decade, it would be wholly within the range of the practical political decisions that need to be made in the United States and in other developed countries.

To forestall the possibility of a successful taxpayers' revolt against this proposal, two points need to be stressed over and over again. First, the cost of assisting in global development must be measured against the eventual cost of *not* doing so—in wars and in a limping world economy (not to mention human suffering or our own dehumanization). Second, so modest a contribution to the well-being of the world could be made up many times over in any one of the following ways: (1) closing tax loopholes; (2) reducing military expenditures; or (3) stimulating the world economy. Regarding the last, development efforts within the United States (the Tennessee Valley Authority, for example, and other public works projects) not only provided jobs for people, but spread benefits through our entire economy. Similarly our aid to Europe after World War II not only helped to resurrect economies there, but it spurred international trade and boosted our own economy. It turned out to be a sound economic investment, just as aid to the developing nations will be, even though the returns will not be as rapid.

CRITERIA FOR ASSISTANCE

What about criteria for the granting of development assistance? It has become increasingly fashionable to argue that they are no longer acceptable or helpful—an easy way out of a difficult responsibility. The fact that donor nations have frequently hindered healthy development by setting misguided criteria for bilateral assistance should not push us in the direction of abandoning standards altogether. These, however, should be arrived at by international agreement and removed from narrow political, military, and economic goals of donor nations—a reason for channeling assistance through international agencies. I suggest the following criteria:

First, need. Under this category, the poorer the country on a per capita basis, the more it would qualify for aid.

Second, capacity for growth. Capacity for growth should indicate much more than how rapidly a country can increase its annual output. Countries would be rated especially on *quality* of growth. Development of food storage facilities or village improvement projects would ordinarily rank high, for example, while production of air conditioners might be counted as having a marginal or negative value. Willingness to initiate responsible economic policies, root out corruption, and take part in regional planning are other examples.

Third, equalization measures. A key requirement for assistance would be a country's willingness to further development in such a way that it produces lasting gains for the masses of bottom-rung poor. It is an intolerable contradiction to infuse a poor country with assistance from wealthy nations, if wealthy people within that poor country are inadequately taxed, or are allowed to send money abroad in large quantities, where it is used to capitalize development in rich nations. Land reform, loans to small farmers, a labor-intensive approach to production, education that includes the rural poor, economic controls, health care and social security, curbs on luxury consumption—these are some of the methods for furthering equalization. The Alliance for Progress was right in proposing reforms toward this end, and wrong in its subsequent failure to insist on them.

Fourth, respect for civil liberties and the practice of democracy. There is no need to underestimate the difficulty of reaching even a limited international agreement on these twin points, but a start would be important. Even then, applying them would require flexibility. For example, as I write these lines, over a third of Africa is under military rule and most of the remaining countries have only one political party; yet the special difficulties they face deserve consideration. Because of tribalism and because their boundaries were arbitrarily drawn by colonial powers, most African states are still struggling to achieve national unity. Nevertheless, after allowances are made for local circumstances, it is still important to distinguish between repressive regimes and those fundamentally committed to the protection of civil liberties and growth in or toward democracy.

Fifth, military spending. Countries whose investment in troops and military hardware clearly exceeds legitimate needs should qualify for less assistance.

Sixth, population control. Again, each country's situation has to be considered; but the population boom is such a fundamental liability to development that we cannot bypass efforts in this area in considering assistance.

No country would have to comply with all six conditions in order to qualify for aid. A formula could be worked out for scaling assistance according to compliance on an overall basis, with each condition having a designated value. States do this now in assistance to public schools. The formula is constantly being improved, but few would argue that we should return to the days of no formula for distributing assistance to schools. A percentage system along the following lines, for example, could indicate the amount of assistance for which a developing country would qualify:

30% Need
20% Capacity for growth
20% Equalization measures
10% Respect for civil liberties
10% Restraint on military spending
10% Population control

This formula is simply a sketch of what needs to be considered. If a poor nation spent excessively on military hardware, it could lose up to 10 percent of its development assistance for that reason alone; but such spending would probably also reduce its capacity for growth and its ability to advance equalization measures, jeopardizing still further the amount of assistance for which it would qualify. A country which promotes population control would receive 10 percent more than one that does not.

This type of economic inducement can give developing nations support to do what they should do on their own, but perhaps for domestic political reasons hesitate to do. When I first served in the Illinois House of Representatives some of the state's best teachers, because they were black, were unable to get jobs, even though we had a serious teacher shortage. I introduced a bill, later enacted, which said that before a school could receive state aid, it had to show that it had not discriminated in the employment of teachers. Suddenly many school superintendents found it both desirable— and politically acceptable to their school boards—to change employment patterns. The motivation may not have been ideal, but the result was good. The same type of situation applies at the international level: the carrot of assistance can help countries adopt better development practices.

If criteria like these are not imposed by a few rich nations, but arranged by consensus among underdeveloped countries and the assisting nations, they would be far less resented than strings attached to present bilateral aid. Further, the criteria I suggest deal with basic development goals. They leave methods open to choice for the most part, permitting each country to decide for itself what is "good" for that country. They do not prescribe capitalism or socialism, for example, but only that development benefit the poor. They allow, by intention, considerable latitude in how a country may go about reaching objectives.

The measurements harmonize with the stated ideals of the United Nations, and they derive no less clearly from the ideals of our own country. Their use would drastically shift the flow of assistance in many instances. Tanzania's efforts to start development with the grass-roots poor would be rewarded far more generously than African states in which corruption and extravagance characterize government officials. India would get a much larger percentage of aid than it now receives, and China could become a recipient nation again. The use of these criteria would put the prestige of world opinion, as well as economic leverage, on the side of desirable policy changes in all underdeveloped countries, and perhaps in the rich countries as well. No formula is foolproof; misjudgments would be inevitable. That should not obscure the fact that without some formula, and the global development effort which it presupposes, the gap between rich and poor is likely to widen catastrophically.

THE RESPONSE OF OTHERS | What if the United States made a wholehearted commitment to a program of international development and a number of rich nations—the Soviet Union and its Eastern European satellites, let us say—did nothing? The question is far from academic, since the Soviets give little economic assistance now and would not be apt to envision successful development, carried out along the lines I have indicated, as conducive to the spread of communism. The Soviet Union might eventually take part, perhaps for positive reasons, but failing that, then perhaps for the negative one of yielding to world opinion. If not, nothing would more dramatically illustrate the strength of democracy. U.S. participation would almost certainly have the impact of drawing a favorable response from rich Western nations and Japan. The response of others should be incidental to our own, in any case, since it is unworthy of us to let the lives of suffering people depend on what other countries may or may not do.

A STRUCTURE FOR DEVELOPMENT | The international community will have to agree on a method of administering an exceedingly complex undertaking, but if a commitment to pool resources and work together emerges, so will a suitable framework.

It makes sense to consider first the use of existing international agencies, especially the United Nations system and the World Bank group. The Pearson report assumes continuation of bilateral assistance, favors its being set within an international framework, and looks primarily to the World Bank group for this. (The Pearson study was sponsored by the World Bank.) Sir Robert Jackson's Capacity Study of the United Nations system, not surprisingly, favors the UN system, but wants it more tightly coordinated. Ninety percent of the money and personnel involved in UN-sponsored activities is already devoted to some form of development. By late 1972 UN agencies working with the UN Development Program were carrying out many of the Jackson study's proposed reforms in order to upgrade their efficiency and increase their capacity to perform. Still, deep skepticism remains regarding the capacity of the UN system, as presently constituted, to effectively administer a greatly expanded development program.

The UN Development Program is already the central international agency for preinvestment and technical assistance. The World Bank group, on the other hand, is the major lending agency, and has steadily broadened its scope to include a wide range of development activities. Preferences as to which organization—or whether a new International Development Authority—should become the chief administrative agency for an expanded and integrated development system might hinge on the fact that in the United Nations underdeveloped countries hold a majority of the votes, while they have 35 percent of the voting rights in the World Bank. Many of them find that unacceptable. A formula needs to be worked out so both rich and poor nations have confidence that sound decisions are made, relatively free from political pressure.

Whatever the structural mechanisms, the expertise that national and international agencies have accumulated can be utilized. The same applies to voluntary agencies, whose growth can be a vital part of world development. Several European countries carry out some government-funded projects through churches because of the latter's long experience and close ties in underdeveloped countries. The United States does this extensively in the case of food relief through P.L. 480. It makes some sense to use the best available channels, and in many cases that will mean voluntary organizations, universities, scientific organizations, or private businesses.

To those who object that such a program moves us in the direction of a world order, the reply is: none too soon. The alternative to world order is world disorder. In fact, the world is already moving toward global systems, where the welfare of all is at stake. In communication by satellite, in control of the environment, in control and use of the seas and seabeds, and in other ways as well, international systems are emerging that transcend political boundaries. Although nationalism seems natural to us, we forget that the nation-state emerged recently, in the modern era of history. National loyalties had to be contrived, fought for, and finally established against all the lesser loyalties that resisted it. This process is still taking place in much of the world. But nationalism without a wider sense of responsibility for the common good is a liability. If nations, recognizing their interdependence, work together to insure that hunger and poverty do not grind half or more of the human race into madness or despair, they are in effect agreeing to move beyond unbridled nationalism. Perhaps this will encourage us to place some of our security problems in the hands of an international peace-keeping force, and to depend more on international law and the International Court of Justice to settle disputes. All of these move us toward a more rational world community, just as an international approach to development does. What kind of future will we invite if we fail to go in this direction?

18

Political Nuts and Bolts

IDEALS AND POLITICAL REALISM

Often economic-assistance goals are drawn by donor nations on the basis of a political realism that at root is cynical and largely divorced from humanitarian ideals. That fact is not always apparent because political leaders customarily package cynical, short-range programs in religious and moral rhetoric—a contradiction that explains in part why so many people have turned away in disgust from politics, and why some have even turned against our system.

Those who espouse political realism want to reject a moralistic approach which demands utopian results, or which tends to see the United States crusading as the children of light against the children of darkness. Such an approach leads to misguided efforts that are not only dangerous, but likely to disillusion people through failure. Against this, realism in politics obviously supplies a healthy dose of caution. But political realism fails precisely the test of realism, if it avoids coming to terms with insistent needs, and if it does not take into account the yearning of many people to help their fellowman. Gunnar Myrdal has stressed that idealistic motives behind assistance can be a powerful incentive: "When some of my colleagues believe that they are particularly hard-boiled and scientific in excluding from their analysis the fact that people plead to their consciences, I believe that they are simply unrealistic."

In the interest of realism, it is important that we draw more fully on humanitarian ideals. Doing so is not simple, however. Take religion, for example.

Because religion is used to support and sanction the social order, we easily forget that a crucial purpose, historically, of the Jewish and Christian traditions is to criticize the social order and hold it responsible for the achievement of justice. The studies of sociologists Glock and Stark have documented this forgetfulness of ours, showing that churchgoers in the United States tend to be more prejudiced and less humanitarian than non-churchgoers, especially when conservative religious beliefs are held. Two other sociologists, Allen and Spilka, have modified this conclusion by distinguishing between "the committed religious" and "the consensual religious." The committed religious think of their faith in terms of relationships, can explain it with clarity, and show in daily activities and in attempts to understand complex issues that it is of central importance to them. The consensual religious think of their faith in terms of specific dos and don'ts, are vague and simplistic in explaining it, and rarely apply it to daily activities. Two-thirds of the latter were found to be prejudiced, while only one in ten of the committed religious fell into that category.

This indicates that a mindless attachment to religion is worse than none at all, serving to harden people against a sympathy for others, while a more thoughtful commitment provides strong motivation for social justice. It suggests that by invoking generalized religion, political leaders may be reinforcing opposition to social justice. It also suggests the importance of communicating to Christians and Jews the essential, not optional, place that justice for poor people has throughout both Old and New Testaments. I stress the word "essential" because the belief that "the earth is the Lord's" and that its fruits are meant to be shared with the least of our human brothers is embedded in the law, the prophets, and the gospels; and it grows out of the central events of faith for Jews and Christians: the Passover-Exodus experience; and the life, death, and resurrection of Jesus.

I single out the religious factor not because humanitarian ideals are absent outside the religious communities—they obviously are not—but because most U.S. citizens claim religious membership, and almost all claim a religious preference. Clearly if they took their underpinnings seriously and would apply these to world hunger in the 1970s, they could rapidly move the nation to assume a major role in global development.

This is not happening because religion has been largely "privatized." Many people in my own denomination (Lutheran) tend to think that although their faith has some bearing on personal matters—how they get along with others, take care of their families, and the like—it has little or no place in forming attitudes about the way society is governed. "The church should stay out of politics and stick to the gospel," I hear them say. It usually reflects an inability to apply the parable of the Good Samaritan to the modern world. Today most people's welfare is extensively determined by impersonal arrangements over which they have little or no control. To turn our backs on making those arrangements more fair is to turn our backs on hungry people and to condemn them to further misery. The privatizing of religion explains why church life in the United States is highly relevant in some ways, but at the same time (considering the church's size) largely irrelevant in terms of helping to bring about a more just social order.

Religion is not unique in fostering a privatized social understanding. Much of our population's outlook is rooted in eighteenth- and nineteenth-century liberalism, with its almost singular emphasis on the autonomy of the individual, and this has privatized our way of life. Economic thinking continues to emphasize individual autonomy, even though the movement toward larger and less personal companies tends to make much of the language meaningless. Psychiatrist Robert Coles says that his profession reflects privatized thinking, too. He points out that people just do not go to psychiatrists to be cured of racial prejudices or of a wish to see this country destroy another country, although such attitudes reflect profound psychological disturbances.

Whether religious or secular, a privatized approach to the world leads to noninvolvement in the social order. But noninvolvement really means throwing your weight on the side of those who oppose change and who therefore defend injustice. Even when a privatized approach motivates people to do works of mercy, it can still accomplish mischief. Because charitable deeds can salve a person's conscience, they may relieve him of feeling responsible for seeking social changes. If so, he may help the poor, but reinforce poverty. Along a similar line, it is ironic that the population explosion, and with it the spread of hunger, are caused partly by deep human concern which brought death control to poor people all over the globe through medicine and public health programs. The commitment of a relatively small number of people is required to reduce the death rate, and unless greater efforts are exerted to help the social and political order catch up, the long-range consequences can only be disastrous.

Fortunately churches and private agencies are turning away from an exclusively relief-oriented approach to hunger, and toward development projects that serve as models for what could be done on a much broader scale. Along with this the thinking of the churches increasingly accepts the necessity of expressing ideals in the arenas of politics and economics. Virtually every large Protestant denomination, the three major branches of Judaism, the World Council of Churches, and the Roman Catholic Church reflect this. I have already cited the example of the papal encyclical, *Development of the Peoples,* in this regard. More recently Pope Paul wrote an apostolic letter on social justice, an excerpt from which illustrates how he relates a traditional faith to the struggle for a just social order:

Animated by the power of the Spirit of Jesus Christ, the Savior of mankind, and upheld by hope, the Christian involves himself in the building up of the human city, one that is to be peaceful, just and fraternal and acceptable as an offering to God. In fact, "the expectation of a new earth must not weaken but rather stimulate our concern for cultivating this one. . . ."

In general, religious leadership is ahead of the people in the pews on this issue, but the people are catching up, and that holds encouragement for a hungry world.

Those who build on secular humanitarian ideals have moved along paths similar to the one I have mentioned for religious groups. They, too, have moral resources to draw on, not the least of which are those embodied in the vision upon which this nation was founded. In any case, humanitarian ideals, whether religiously motivated or not, will have to supply much of the impetus if global development is to take place. That is political realism.

THE CASE FOR A NEW MOVEMENT

Hunger makes heady politics. Several decades ago a young student came to Santiago, Chile, to study medicine. With other medical students he lived in poor neighborhoods near the school where "we learned very quickly that good health is something you buy, and many people cannot pay the price." He got a job performing autopsies in a public hospital, and later observed that "when one must perform autopsies one becomes aware of the physiological misery of some people, of what hunger does to people and of the extraordinary difference between those who can pay for a private clinic and those who live poorly, get sick and die in a public hospital." Today that former medical student is Salvador Allende, Marxist President of Chile.

Understandably, hunger abroad can breed radical politics—there. It is less clear, however, what impact, if any, a hungry world can have on the United States. That it *should* change political priorities for us is abundantly clear. But can it?

I am prepared to argue that it can—that enough U.S. citizens are favorably conditioned, or could rapidly become so, to bring about a national commitment, legislated in Congress, to reduce hunger and poverty in the world through a massive, internationally sponsored development effort. Doing this probably requires a widespread political movement, because not only must public opinion be aroused, but that opinion has to be translated into national legislation. This will not happen without controversy and without extensive grass-roots activity. The struggle demands deeply committed people who are willing to stick doggedly to this issue.

Is that kind of political movement plausible?

It would be easy to assemble a persuasive case against that possibility. Our national leadership has stood in the way for the past decade. No candidate sees world hunger or global development as vote-getters. Senator George McGovern, the Democratic nominee for President in 1972, understands well the problem of world hunger—he headed the Food for Peace program under John F. Kennedy—and during the 1972 campaign he delivered a major foreign policy statement entitled "A New Internationalism." It was an eloquent statement of the need for U.S. partnership in world development with the hungry majority. Despite the importance of that statement, it received only passing attention and was ignored by President Nixon.

Few candidates for Congress address themselves with such honesty to global human needs. Many of them know the needs, but they also know that candidates who want to win have to touch the immediate concerns of their electorate. This simply reflects a basic characteristic of politics: it is a short-range enterprise. Politics tends to get preoccupied with day-to-day problems rather than to anticipate needs or search for long-term solutions. The public, by pursuing its own immediate self-interest, pressures leaders to courses of action which are irrational because they neglect or undermine distant goals.

Where are the constituents favoring global development? Sharecroppers in India, illiterate peasants in Ghana, and hungry, sickly

children in Peru have no political clout in the United States. They
cannot vote for a more effective Congress or even lobby to make
their plight understood. Perhaps the universities could be expected
to raise an articulate and sizable voice on their behalf, but not so.
In 1969 James P. Grant, President of the Overseas Development
Council, noted the irony that

. . . many of the "concerned" students of today will have little or
nothing to do with U.S. development assistance programs . . . no students have seized a university building to protest the almost unbeliev-
able lack of courses in most universities tailored to equip them to
participate in the world-wide fight against poverty and social injustice.
Nor have any students picketed the Congress for its slashing of hundreds of millions of dollars of funds needed to fuel the development
breakthrough. . . .

Grant was hardly advising students to seize buildings—a method
more apt to arouse public hostility than win support. But he does
underscore the fact that, far from becoming advocates for the hungry half of the world, our colleges and universities have responded
with eloquent silence. One can detect in this and in much of the
peace movement generally a moral schizophrenia, for we are left to
infer that while killing people through war is an outrage against
humanity, letting them starve to death is perfectly all right.

Despite formidable obstacles to launching a movement for
global development, I believe such a movement can and must take
place. Our disengagement from Vietnam presents a ripe occasion
for reexamining our foreign policy in general, and our way of
relating to underdeveloped countries in particular. Even if we
begin to concentrate solely and successfully on our most distressing
domestic problems, we may, a decade from now, still find ourselves turned inward as a nation, more hardened than ever against
hunger and poverty in the world. And if we reach out then, it may
be too late. Global development is so urgent that we cannot risk
putting it off.

Many say that the defeat of George McGovern in the 1972
presidential race shows that the spark of idealism has escaped the

electorate. I disagree. As the Illinois chairman for the McGovern campaign, I think I got a reasonably accurate sense of what happened. How people perceived the candidates as presidential timber, rather than the issues, dominated that election. Those of us who supported George McGovern—and the candidate himself—did not get across to the people the kind of man he is. But the positions McGovern took on most key issues reflected the sentiments of a public majority, or at least reflected viewpoints that a majority would have been willing to follow. If his stance toward the hungry world garnered few votes, neither did it arouse public opposition.

Pitted against U.S. workers, farmers, and business leaders, a movement for global development is sure to fail. But made in concert with domestic reforms, such as guaranteed work (which would help stabilize business and farm income), a movement to help the hungry can gain support from a great cross-section of citizens. An emphasis on feeding the hungry abroad should add to, rather than detract from, efforts to raise people above the level of hunger in the United States.

I believe we can also take advantage of spreading dissatisfaction with politics as a short-run, ineffective enterprise. C. P. Snow has said that healthy people and healthy societies have "an appetite for the future." As the consequences of our failure to bring about a more just social order in the world become more apparent, and the possibilities of rational alternatives also surface, we can at least hope for a more enlightened understanding of self-interest. Because the long-range crisis of hunger and poverty is becoming less long-range, the broken future which it promises our children is becoming more clear, and the possibilities of assembling significant public pressure for rational responses increase. In 1969 UN Secretary-General U Thant said:

I do not wish to seem overdramatic, but I can only conclude from the information available to me as Secretary-General that the members of the United Nations have perhaps ten years left in which to subordinate their ancient quarrels and launch a global partnership to curb the arms race, to improve the human environment, to defuse the population explosion, and to supply the required momentum to world development efforts.

If such an appeal is negative and alarmist, it can still prompt action, just as the spread of disease to the rich spurred public health measures in the last century.

There is a more positive side to our widespread disaffection with politics as usual. Perhaps it could be described as an instinctive human urge to engage in world-building: to construct mentally and participate in a view of the world that makes sense because it works and offers meaning. Through the centuries nations have manipulated this urge for the purpose of waging war, summoning people to offer themselves in dramatic confrontation. That willingness to sacrifice—life itself in the case of war—must now be harnessed for reducing hunger and poverty. Although neither hunger nor poverty is as dramatic as war, can we spread the conviction that feeding hungry people is a world-building enterprise at least as worthy of sacrifice?

Politics is prone to have a short-range outlook, but dissatisfaction with it has deep and growing roots that can serve as the basis for change. That basis rests in part on a broader conception of self-interest, and in part on humanitarian ideals. In terms of development a focus on hunger helps, because people understand deeply personal needs and immediate benefits. George McGovern has pointed out that while foreign aid was unpopular and controversial, feeding the hungry was, ironically, popular both in Congress and among the U.S. public.

A survey late in 1972 by the Gallup organization—called "an exhaustive poll" by *Time* magazine—showed only 24 percent of the public supporting economic aid to foreign countries. But another professional public opinion survey, authorized by the American Freedom from Hunger Foundation and other groups, and released early in 1973, showed substantially more sentiment for helping hungry people beyond our borders. In fact the second survey found that among those under 30, world hunger is the number one social-political concern. It is one of the disconcerting contradictions in public opinion today, that many oppose "foreign economic assistance" but favor "helping the hungry in other nations."

From this it is reasonable to conclude that if economic assistance and a program for global development were presented as enabling people to rise above the level of hunger, it could strike a responsive chord across this land.

When we ask why university students have not led national mobilizations for world development, some offer the understandable excuse that Vietnam and Cold War abuses have turned them against foreign aid. But should we object to a war which threatens some of us and kills hundreds of people a day, but not object to hunger and poverty which daily destroy by the thousands? If so, moral bankruptcy is more widespread than the peace movement has charged. If not, development for the hungry will be seized as a positive alternative to military excesses abroad. I am willing to bet that this positive alternative will attract many who opposed—as well as many who supported—the war in Vietnam. One indication of that may be the "Hikes for the Hungry" (now, significantly, called "Walks for Development"), sponsored by the American Freedom from Hunger Foundation, in which hundreds of thousands of youths have taken part—precisely the sort of interest that could provide raw material for a serious political enterprise. Those walks developed more than blisters. On one of the hikes in which I participated, a television newsman was interviewing me and then suddenly thrust the mike at a twelve-year-old boy standing next to me. "Why are you making this hike?" he asked. "Because I want to help hungry people," the youth replied. My guess is that the boy's investment in time and energy helped to shape a lasting attitude, and when he is twenty-five he will still be ready to make sacrifices for hungry people—sacrifices that he may also be able to channel through the political process.

The importance of appealing to humanitarian ideals should not be underrated, especially with students and young adults. The absence of such an appeal will only prompt highly motivated people to look elsewhere. One historian has written this about the Weimar Republic:

The main weakness of the moderate Socialists and the German liberals was that they lacked not just inspired leadership, but the courage of their convictions. . . . Unlike the Nazis and the Communists, they had no ideas, no faith or promise to offer to the young generation, only the sober, reasonable, unemotional, and tired explanation that democracy was probably the least oppressive of all political systems. This was not very satisfactory for a young generation in search of the Holy Grail.

At the same time, those who build on humanitarian ideals need to steer people away from undue optimism. The idea of human progress, rooted in the accomplishments of science and technology, and in the settling of new lands over the past several centuries, has given the West in general and citizens of our country in particular a faith in success. We expect to win all wars, arrive first on the moon, prosper and be happy, and we become frustrated if these things do not happen. This attitude reflects an inordinate trust in science, technology, hard work, and sincerity. While optimism up to a point is a positive motivater, beyond that point it becomes counterproductive. When China fell to the communists, it was inconceivable to much of the U.S. public that this could possibly have happened—to us! Some of our most respected leaders, along with U.S. China experts who anticipated this twist of history and tried to explain it, became scapegoats. This atmosphere prevented us from examining developments like those in Vietnam in a detached and rational manner.

Idealists often indulge in excessive optimism, perhaps in part because they tend to be young and limited in experience. Many idealists give their souls to a cause in the hope of achieving rapid and complete reform. When this does not happen, they lose patience and fall away, feeling that the system has let them down. Undue optimism not only programs people for failure, it also makes them vulnerable to despair, incapable of assisting in moderate changes.

In the case of support for global development, inflated optimism does not come to terms with the need to engage in a long, obstinate struggle. Gains against world hunger require humble sacrifices and promise few heroic victories. I stress this because the most characteristic weakness of political reform movements is that they seldom develop, from the grass-roots level on up, the kind of hard-nosed commitment to grubby, undramatic work over the long pull—organizing, knocking on doors, writing letters, and boning up on the issues. Unfortunately, crusaders tend to substitute a sense of moral superiority for hard work. But if less idealistic people have a bigger hand in shaping political decisions because they devote themselves to the nuts and bolts of grass-roots politics, reformers have no one to blame but themselves. When idealists commit themselves to the same hard work, their influence expands accordingly.

If the United States is to support a more intensive global development program, then among those recruited to work for such support will have to be large numbers of people who are already committed to sharing with the poor, but who are accustomed to expressing this exclusively through direct gifts to persons or to private relief organizations. I hasten to stress that I do not pit political action against private assistance. On the contrary. Just as I believe a political movement for global development would spur private contributions, I also want those who help through private organizations to translate this concern into the broader and more comprehensive channel of action by government. That can change a personal concern into a national commitment.

Relief agencies do, as a natural by-product, condition many citizens for support of foreign economic assistance. They may be timid about making that encouragement explicit, however, for fear of undercutting their own ability to raise funds—an unwarranted fear, I believe—and on some occasions even exploit antipathy to government assistance. (One agency, whose work I respect, promotes itself through an advertisement that pictures an aged recipient from Brazil. The ad has the heading, "This woman could wreck our Foreign Aid Program." It concludes, "If you are tired of seeing your hard-earned dollars earn so few returns overseas, yet you want to share your blessings with the less fortunate—then you are invited to write [name of agency] today.") On the whole, however, relief agencies are becoming more sensitive to the fact that unless comprehensive global development takes place, relief operations represent little more than an exercise in futility. I would like to see these organizations enter more boldly into a movement supporting global development, because they are highly respected and in touch with millions of people already motivated to share with the hungry abroad. These donors could form an impressive new vanguard for revamping the nation's relationship to the impoverished of the world.

I have indicated that churches are gradually encouraging people away from a privatized way of relating to society. The involvement of religious people in this political task is absolutely essential. For example, if one Sunday morning churches across the land had a special offering, not of money, but of letters to congressmen from lay members who spelled out in personal terms their desire to see the United States share with the world's hungry through global development; and if that modest offering were followed by active local committees who carried out a long-range grass-roots strategy for bringing this about, we would soon see visible results in Washington. Such support by the churches becomes increasingly possible as members perceive that to be "above politics" on this issue is also to be above religion, and to lobby for the spread of hunger.

I would like to see John W. Gardner's Common Cause support global development as one of its key goals. This effective national citizens' lobby, which aims at "the rebuilding of this nation," has understandably concentrated its first two years on domestic issues. But I believe that separated from global imperatives, the rebuilding of the United States is destined to assume grotesque proportions. It is urgent that Common Cause soon help to get this nation behind global development.

In short, I am arguing that, if we are to have a livable world, not only is an assault on world hunger through comprehensive development essential, but the politics of getting U.S. backing for such an undertaking is within reach. A broad enough base of support already exists to force an extended national debate on the issue. And if the proposed stance of the United States toward the world that I have outlined were clearly placed in harmony with a program to resolve our own development problems, then a coalition of interests favoring global development could become a new majority, able once again to have this country keep faith with its founding vision.

Acknowledgments

This manuscript would not have been possible without help from many people, in and out of government, only a few of whom are acknowledged here. We would like to single out those who read all or parts of the manuscript and offered valuable suggestions, including Barry Commoner, Irving Dilliard, Martin E. Marty, Harold Remus, Henry S. Reuss, Arthur M. Schlesinger, Jr., Harry Succop, and Leroy Wehrle. Our mother, Mrs. Martin P. Simon, typed the manuscript. Sylvia Davis and Ray Johnsen helped in other ways. Our wives, Jeanne and Kaiya, gave more than ordinary assistance. We are grateful to all of these people without holding any of them responsible for our conclusions.

P.S. and A.S.

Notes

Chapter 1: Establishing a Point of View

Page 8. Weitz quotation: Charles H. Weitz, "Action for Development," *War on Hunger,* January, 1971.

Page 10. McNamara quotation: from a report to the Board of Governors of the International Bank for Reconstruction and Development, September 21, 1970.

Pages 10–11. The Snow address is published under the title *The State of Siege* (New York: Scribner's, 1969).

Chapter 2: The Hungry Majority

Page 24. Jackson quotation: Jesse L. Jackson, letter to Gov. Richard B. Ogilvie, May 19, 1969, in *Nutrition and Human Needs: Part 10— SCLC and East St. Louis,* Hearings before the Select Committee on Nutrition and Human Needs of the U.S. Senate, p. 3265.

Page 25. van den Heuvel quotation: from *The Development Apocalypse,* edited by Stephen C. Rose and Peter Paul van Lelyveld (New York: National Council of Churches, 1967), p. 157.

Page 26. Thomsen quotations: Moritz Thomsen, *Living Poor* (Seattle: University of Washington Press, 1969), pp. 83–84, 273–74.

Page 29. Boerma quotation: from a foreword to *The State of Food and Agriculture 1971,* published by FAO.

Page 31. Black quotation: from the foreword to Lester R. Brown's *Seeds of Change* (New York: Praeger, 1970).

Page 32. Study on Asian productivity over 50-year period: cited by René Dumont in *The Hungry Future,* by Dumont and Paul Rosier (New York: Praeger, 1969), p. 205.

Page 33. The New York Times: article by Sydney H. Schanberg, March 11, 1971.

Pages 34–35. Study of West Pakistan town near Lahore: reported in *The New York Times,* October 25, 1970.

Page 35. Topping quotation: The New York Times, June 25, 1971.

Page 35. Snow quotation: Edgar Snow, "Aftermath of the Cultural Revolution," *The New Republic,* April 10, 1971.

Pages 36–37. The Times of London study: cited by Anthony Lewis in *The New York Times,* May 1, 1971.

Page 37. The Pretoria study: cited by J. V. O. Reid in *Reality,* July, 1970, and reprinted in the *Congressional Record,* September 16, 1970, by Congressman Charles C. Diggs, Jr.

Page 40. Berg quotation: Alan Berg, "Industry's struggle with world malnutrition," *Harvard Business Review,* January–February, 1972.

Page 44. Boerma quotation: Addeke H. Boerma, keynote address to the Second World Food Congress, The Hague, June 16, 1970.

Chapter 3: The Poor Have More

Page 46. Quotation on Calcutta: Philip Appleman, *The Silent Explosion* (Boston: Beacon Press, 1965), pp. 3, 7.

Page 47. Brown quotation: The Population Reference Bureau's *Population Bulletin,* December, 1969, p. 134.

Pages 47–48. Viel quotation: Benjamin Viel, "The Social Consequences of Population Growth," Population Reference Bureau, October, 1969.

Pages 53–54. Statistics on India from 1891 to 1951: Carlo M. Cipolla, *The Economic History of World Population* (Baltimore: Penguin Books, 1970), p. 91.

Pages 54–55. Canadian writer quotation: Mervyn Jones, *Two Ears of Corn* (London: Hodder and Stoughton, 1966), pp. 72–73.

Page 55. Moraes quotations: Dom Moraes, "Bombay," *The New York Times Magazine,* October 11, 1970.

Page 56. India's Minister of State for Family Planning: S. Chandrasekhar in an address to the Second World Food Congress, The Hague, June 24, 1970.

Page 58. Figures on South Korea, Taiwan and Brazil: William Rich, "Smaller Families Through Jobs and Justice," *International Development Review,* Vol. XIV, No. 3, 1972–73.

Pages 59–60. The Pearson report: Partners in Development: Report of the Commission on International Development, Lester B. Pearson, Chairman (New York: Praeger, 1969), p. 57.

Page 60. Aguirre quotation: Alfredo Aguirre, "Colombia: The Family in Candelaría," in *Studies in Family Planning,* April, 1966, a publication of The Population Council.

Page 61. Viel quotation: cited above.

Page 62. Commoner quotation: Barry Commoner, *The Closing Circle* (New York: Knopf, 1972), pp. 243–44.

Pages 63–64. On U.S. population distribution: see James L. Sundquist's essay, "Where Shall They Live?" reprinted by The Brookings Institution from *The Public Interest,* Winter, 1970.

Page 64. The National Goals Research Staff was a White House group formed by President Nixon and directed by Leonard Garment. Its findings were published by the Government Printing Office on July 4, 1970, under the title, *Toward Balanced Growth: Quantity with Quality,* from which this quotation came.

Page 65. Mayer quotation: Jean Mayer, "Toward a Non-Malthusian Population Policy," *The Columbia Forum,* Summer, 1969.

Page 66. Morris quotation: Morris is quoted by C. P. Gilmore, "Something Better Than the Pill?" in *The New York Times Magazine,* July 20, 1969.

Page 68. Notestein quotation: "Population Growth and Its Control," in *Overcoming World Hunger,* Clifford M. Hardin, editor (Englewood Cliffs, New Jersey: Prentice-Hall, 1969), p. 30.

Page 69. Cooke quotation: in *U.S. Foreign Assistance in the 1970s: A New Approach,* report to the President from the Task Force on International Development, Rudolph A. Peterson, Chairman, March 4, 1970, p. 17, footnote.

Chapter 4: A Widening Gap

Page 71. Drucker quotation: Peter F. Drucker, *Landmarks of Tomorrow* (New York: Harper & Row, 1959), pp. 160–61.

Page 72. Bloodworth quotation: Dennis Bloodworth, *An Eye for the Dragon, Southeast Asia Observed: 1954–1970* (New York: Farrar, Straus & Giroux, 1970), p. 78.

Page 72. Borgstrom quotation: Georg A. Borgstrom, "The Dual Challenge of Health and Hunger—A Global Crisis," Population Reference Bureau, January, 1970.

Page 73. Pearson quotation. Lester B. Pearson, "Conflicting Perspectives on the Development Problem: An Introduction," *Journal of International Affairs,* No. 2, 1970, p. 159.

Page 77. Pearson quotation: ibid., p. 163.

Chapter 5. The Development Struggle

Page 81. Rosier quotation: Dumont and Rosier, as cited, p. 78.

Pages 81–82. Pearson Commission: as cited, p. 11.

Page 86. Pearson report: as cited, p. 54.

Page 88. Watanabe quotation: James P. Sterba, *The New York Times,* August 28, 1972.

Page 89. Pearson report: as cited, p. 67.

Chapter 6: Agricultural Development

Pages 91–92. Johnson quotation: from an address to the Commission on World Hunger of the Lutheran Church—Missouri Synod, September 24, 1970.

Page 92. Borlaug quotation: in an interview with Gerald Leach, "Can World Technology Stave Off Mass Famine?" *Chicago Sun-Times,* April 30, 1972.

Page 92. Dumont quotation: Dumont and Rosier, as cited, p. 162.

Pages 92–93. Study of Ministers of Agriculture: William and Paul Paddock, *Famine 1975!* (Boston: Little, Brown, 1967), p. 75.

Pages 95–96. "In Taiwan . . ." quotation: James P. Grant, *Economic and Business Outlook for the Developing Countries in the 1970's: Trends and Issues* (Washington: Overseas Development Council, 1970), p. 17.

Chapter 7: Industrial Development

Pages 100–01. Meister on migrating family: Albert Meister, "The Urbanization Crisis of Rural Man," *Ceres,* November–December, 1970.

Page 101. The New York Times on African cities: article by William Borders, April 30, 1971.

Chapter 8: Trade

Page 104. Pearson commission: as cited, p. 45.

Page 105. Pearson quotation: Vernon Duckworth-Barker, *Breakthrough to Tomorrow, The Story of International Co-operation for Development through the United Nations* (New York: United Nations, 1970), pp. 48–49.

Page 106. Grant quotation: as cited, p. 24.

Page 107. Parry on Virginia colony: J. H. Parry, *The Establishment of the European Hegemony: 1415–1715* (New York: Harper & Row, 1961), p. 98.

Chapter 9: Economic Assistance

Page 111. Aquino quotation: from an address to the sixteenth session of the FAO Conference in Rome, November, 1971.

Page 112. Eicher quotation: Carl K. Eicher, "Danger: Underestimating the Population Explosion," *Ceres,* November–December, 1970.

Chapter 10: Models of Development

Page 118. The Wall Street Journal on Brazil: articles by Everett G. Martin, April 14 and 21, 1972.

Page 120. Saar quotation: "A Whole Country Being Worked Very Hard," *Life,* April 30, 1971.

Page 120. Dumont quotation: Dumont and Rosier, as cited, p. 133.

Pages 120–21. One observer quotation: John W. Gurley, "The New Man in the New China," *Center Magazine,* May, 1970.

Page 121. Cooray quotation: from an address, "The Church and Economic Problems in Asia," Manila, November 24, 1970.

Page 126. Schanberg quotation: The New York Times, March 11, 1971.

Chapter 11: Food or Clean Air?

Pages 130–31. Beaufort County: see Arthur Simon, "Battle of Beaufort," *The New Republic,* May 23, 1970.

Page 131. Black delegates' statement: Population Reference Bureau's Population Bulletin, December, 1970, pp. 18–19.

Page 131. Hauser quotation: ibid., p. 20.

Page 133. Environment symposium quotations: reported by Jerry M. Flint, *The New York Times,* June 21, 1970.

Page 138. Hoffman quotation: from his farewell address as Administrator of the UN Development Program, delivered on October 14, 1971, to the UN General Assembly (Second Committee).

Page 138. Commoner quotation: as cited, p. 141.

Page 138. "Ecological wisdom . . ." quotation: Barry Commoner, as cited, pp. 289–90.

Page 141. Commoner quotation: Barry Commoner, "Motherhood in Stockholm," *Harper's Magazine,* June, 1972.

Chapter 12: The Rediscovery of America

Pages 148–49. Myrdal quotations: Gunnar Myrdal, *Asian Drama: An Inquiry into the Poverty of Nations* (New York: Pantheon, 1968), volume I, pp. 169–71.

Page 149. Roosevelt quotation: cited by J. William Fulbright, *The Arrogance of Power* (New York: Vintage Books, 1966), p. 115.

Page 149. Marshall warning: reported by *The New York Times,* June 25, 1972, based on a volume of classified documents that had just been released by the State Department.

Page 151. Stans quotation: The New York Times, April 24, 1971.

Pages 151–52. Fulbright quotation: The Arrogance of Power, as cited, p. 85.

Chapter 13: Trade, Free and Fair

Page 155. Estimate of cost to U.S. consumers: Malmgren and Kimmins, Overseas Development Council report, *World Trade: Engine for Global Progress,* revised, March 1972.

Page 156. "Our policy . . ." quotation: David Ross, "New Hope for Latin America?" *The New Republic,* November 22, 1969.

Page 157. The Christian Century quotation: from an editorial, "Nixon and the New, New, New Look of Aid," September 30, 1970.

Pages 157–58. Jessup quotation: Life, March 27, 1970.

Pages 158–59. Journal of Commerce quotation: from an editorial, "Appointment in Santiago (I) Rough Sledding Ahead," March 27, 1972.

Chapter 14: Profits Abroad

Page 162. Myrdal quotation: Gunnar Myrdal, *The Challenge of World Poverty* (New York: Pantheon, 1970), p. 455.

Pages 165–66. The Hirschman essay: published by the International Finance Section, Department of Economics, Princeton University, 1969.

Chapter 15: Foreign Aid: A Case of Intentions

Pages 169–71. Estimating the aid-element of food shipments: making an estimate has its difficulties. For example, when food is bought from us in local currency, and that currency is loaned back to a recipient country for defense purposes, should we regard the total transaction as food or military assistance? With all the factors I mention taken into account, and remembering that most food shipments are now repayable in dollars, it is generous to count 50 percent of the value of Food for Peace shipments as hardcore assistance, I believe. In *The Myth of Aid,* by Denis Goulet and Michael Hudson (Maryknoll, N.Y.: Orbis Books, 1971), pp. 85–92, Michael Hudson analyzes the P.L. 480 program and concludes that it "has been achieved at virtually no economic cost to the United States . . ." James W. Howe writes that "surplus agricultural commodities . . . belong under the budget heading of U.S. farm subsidy rather than foreign aid." *The "Killing" of U.S. Aid to the Poor Countries* (Washington: Overseas Development Council, 1972), p. 9.

Page 170. "Since we have . . ." quotation: James W. Howe, ibid.

Page 173. The Wall Street Journal quotation: November 3, 1971.

Page 173. Forbes report: "Feeding the World's Hungry Millions: How It Will Mean Billions for U.S. Business," March 1, 1966, cited by Michael Harrington, *Toward a Democratic Left* (Baltimore: Penguin, 1969), pp. 170–71.

Page 175. "Business is the only interest group . . ." quotation: Jerome Levinson and Juan de Onís, *The Alliance That Lost Its Way* (Chicago: Quadrangle, 1970), p. 160.

Page 176. Schaetzel quotation: Flora Lewis, *The New York Times,* October 29, 1972.

Page 179. Myrdal quotation: The Challenge of World Poverty, as cited, p. 383.

Page 181. McNamara quotation: quoted in *War on Hunger,* November, 1972.

Chapter 16: Let Them Eat Missiles

Page 185. McNamara quotation: from his report to the Board of Governors of the IBRD, as cited.

Page 187. McNamara quotation: from an interview with Henry Brandon, "Robert McNamara's New Sense of Mission," *The New York Times Magazine,* November 9, 1969.

Pages 187–88. McNamara quotation: ibid.

Page 188. Symington quotations: Stuart Symington, "Congress's Right to Know," *The New York Times Magazine,* August 9, 1970.

Page 189. Ribicoff quotation: from an editorial, "Planning for Peace," *The Progressive,* May, 1961.

Page 191. Laird quotation: February 13, 1969, cited by the office of the Assistant Secretary of Defense in a letter to Arthur Simon, May 9, 1972.

Page 194. Pope Paul VI quotation: from his papal encyclical, *Development of the Peoples,* March 26, 1967.

Chapter 17: Proposal for Global Development

Page 197. Goulet quotation: Denis Goulet, "The Disappointing Decade of Development," *Center Magazine,* September, 1969.

Page 199. Agnew reference: James Reston, *The New York Times,* April 21, 1971.

Page 200. Harrington quotation: as cited, pp. 8–9.

Page 202. Pearson commission quotation: as cited, p. 202.

Page 203. Myrdal quotation: The Challenge of World Poverty, as cited, p. 279.

Page 205. McNamara quotation: address to the Board of Governors of the IBRD, as cited.

Page 205. Pope Paul VI quotation: as cited.

Chapter 18: Political Nuts and Bolts

Page 214. Myrdal quotation: The Challenge of World Poverty, as cited, p. 76.

Page 214. Allen and Spilka reference: R. O. Allen and B. Spilka, "Committed and Consensual Religion: A Specification of Religion-Prejudice Relationships," *Journal for the Scientific Study of Religion,* Fall, 1967, pp. 191–202.

Pages 216–17. Pope Paul IV quotation: Apostolic Letter to Cardinal Maurice Roy, May 14, 1971, on the 80th anniversary of the encyclical *Rerum Novarum.*

Page 217. Allende quotation: Norman Gall, "The Chileans Have Elected a Revolution," *The New York Times Magazine,* November 1, 1970.

Page 219. Grant quotation: James P. Grant, "President Nixon's Strange Dilemma and His Unprecedented Opportunity," *International Development Review,* June, 1969.

Pages 220–21. U Thant quotation: from an address at the opening conference on "The Second United Nations Development Decade: A Challenge for Rich and Poor Countries," sponsored by the Institute on Man and Science, May 9, 1969, at the United Nations.

Page 223. Weimar Republic quotation: Walter Laqueur, "A look back at the Weimar Republic—The Cry was, 'Down With Das System'," *The New York Times Magazine,* August 16, 1970.

Index

239

ABOUT THE AUTHORS | PAUL SIMON is a weekly newspaper publisher by background, who served fourteen years in the Illinois House and Senate, plus four years as Lieutenant Governor. An independent Democrat, he won national recognition for his work as a legislator. He is the author of five previous books, including *A Hungry World* and *Lincoln's Preparation for Greatness,* the only major scholarly study of Lincoln's years in the Illinois House of Representatives. He has traveled abroad frequently to familiarize himself with conditions in other countries. At age forty-four Simon now heads a graduate program of public affairs reporting at Sangamon State University in Springfield, Illinois, and is currently a fellow at the John F. Kennedy Institute of Politics at Harvard University.

ARTHUR SIMON, a Lutheran clergyman, has served a parish on the Lower East Side of Manhattan since 1961. His previous books include *Faces of Poverty* and *Stuyvesant Town USA: Pattern For Two Americas,* and he has written for *The Atlantic Monthly, Commonweal, The New Republic,* and other journals. At present he is helping to organize Bread for the World, a citizens' lobby against world hunger and poverty.

73 74 75 76 77 10 9 8 7 6 5 4 3 2 1